D0072959

Flappers

Guides to
Subcultures and
Countercultures

Flappers
A Guide to an American Subculture

Kelly Boyer Sagert

GREENWOOD PRESS
An Imprint of ABC-CLIO, LLC

A B C ☙ C L I O

Santa Barbara, California • Denver, Colorado • Oxford, England

Library of Congress Cataloging-in-Publication Data

Sagert, Kelly Boyer.
    Flappers : a guide to an American subculture / Kelly Boyer Sagert.
        p. cm.—(Guides to subcultures and countercultures)
    Includes bibliographical references and index.
        ISBN 978-0-313-37690-0 (hbk. : alk. paper) — ISBN 978-0-313-37691-7 (ebook)
    1. Women—United States—History—20th century. 2. Women—United States—Social life and customs—History—20th century. 3. Women—United States—Social conditions—History—20th century. 4. Nineteen twenties. 5. Popular culture—United States—History—20th century. 6. United States—Social life and customs—1918–1945. I. Title.
    HQ1420.S24   2010
    305.242'2097309042—dc22   2009035383

ISBN: 978-0-313-37690-0
EISBN: 978-0-313-37691-7

14   13   12   11   10   1   2   3   4   5

This book is also available on the World Wide Web as an eBook.
Visit www.abc-clio.com for details.

Greenwood Press
An Imprint of ABC-CLIO, LLC

ABC-CLIO, LLC
130 Cremona Drive, P.O. Box 1911
Santa Barbara, California 93116-1911

This book is printed on acid-free paper (∞)

Manufactured in the United States of America

To my niece, Erin Nicole, who is intelligent, beautiful, and athletic—and who has inspired me countless times with her double thumbs-up gesture and these four words: "Remember, Kelly . . . Girl Power!"

Contents

Series Foreword

From Beatniks to Flappers, Zoot Suiters to Punks, this series brings to life some of the most compelling countercultures in American history. Designed to offer a quick, in-depth examination and current perspective on each group, the series aims to stimulate the reader's understanding of the richness of the American experience. Each book explores a countercultural group critical to American life and introduces the reader to its historical setting and precedents, the ways in which it was subversive or countercultural, and its significance and legacy in American history. *Webster's Ninth New Collegiate Dictionary* defines counterculture as "a culture with values and mores that run counter to those of established society." Although some of the groups covered can be described as primarily subcultural, they were targeted for inclusion because they have not existed in a vacuum. They have advocated for rules that methodically opposed mainstream culture, or they have lived by their ideals to the degree that it became impossible not to impact the society around them. They have left their marks, both positive and negative, on the fabric of American culture. Volumes cover such groups as Hippies and Beatniks, who impacted popular culture, literature, and art; the Eco-Socialists and Radical

Feminists, who worked toward social and political change; and even groups such as the Ku Klux Klan, who left mostly scars.

A lively alternative to narrow historiography and scholarly monographs, each volume in the *Subcultures and Countercultures* series can be described as a "library in a book," containing both essays and browsable reference materials, including primary documents, to enhance the research process and bring the content alive in a variety of ways. Written for students and general readers, each volume includes engaging illustrations, a timeline of critical events in the subculture, topical essays that illuminate aspects of the subculture, a glossary of subculture terms and slang, biographical sketches of the key players involved, and primary source excerpts—including speeches, writings, articles, first-person accounts, memoirs, diaries, government reports, and court decisions—that offer contemporary perspectives on each group. In addition, each volume includes an extensive bibliography of current recommended print and nonprint sources appropriate for further research.

Preface

Sandwiched between the bloody First World War and the suffering of the Great Depression was the pleasure-seeking decade of the 1920s. Labeled as the Roaring Twenties, the Jazz Age, and the Boom Era, this decade witnessed a whirlwind of social change, especially for women. For the first time ever, a significant percentage of young women embraced the flapper lifestyle, which included dresses cut up to their knees; shiny hair bobbed to their chins; and impudent slang, as they indulged in drinking, smoking, and petting. More women lived in cities than ever before, and they worked outside the home in increasing numbers, earning their own incomes and garnering a sense of independence and economic power not seen in previous generations.

During this decade, the first radio broadcast was heard; by the decade's end cars had gone from being a luxury of the few to something 122 million people owned; women were granted the right to vote; and Americans were denied the ability to legally manufacture, transport, distribute, or sell alcoholic beverages, among other happenings of cultural significance.

Flappers provides an in-depth look at the era of flappers, examining the lives of movie stars and screenwriters, musicians and novelists, gangsters and more who lived, worked, loved, and played during the 1920s. Biographies range from those of flapper actresses of significance—Clara Bow, Colleen Moore, and Olive Thomas—to musicians such as George Gershwin, Duke Ellington, and Bessie Smith; a gangster who profited immeasurably during Prohibition; a young teacher who was tried in court for teaching evolution in the classroom, which sparked national debate and heated controversy; and more.

This book also contains essays that focus on one particular aspect of the flapper subculture, ranging from silent and "talkie" films to Prohibition, and from the flapper as a modern woman to the contributions made by F. Scott and Zelda Fitzgerald, as well as a historical overview of the era from a contemporary perspective and another analyzing the origins, impact, and consequences of the subculture.

Included in this book are nine intriguing articles of the 1920s from primary sources that focus on the shocking scandals of the day—including those involving Roscoe "Fatty" Arbuckle and William Desmond Taylor—and the opinions about flappers, both pro and con, including those of Hollywood's "Golden Couple," Mary Pickford and Douglas Fairbanks Sr. Each primary source article starts with a succinct section of text putting the article into context.

Flappers also contains a timeline of the flapper subculture and a glossary of subculture slang, along with scattered sidebars highlighting anecdotes and facts that spotlight certain aspects of American life in the 1920s, and a general bibliography.

The Roaring Twenties and the age of the flappers effectively ended when the stock market crashed on October 24, 1929, but the influence of this era lives on, especially in the lives of women who gained significantly more freedom during this controversial decade—and their daughters and granddaughters who have reaped the benefits of these sweeping social changes.

Timeline

April 6, 1917	The United States enters into the world war being fought in Europe; as men leave to fight overseas, more women are needed in the workplace and to volunteer for the Red Cross and other charitable organizations.
1918	The head of the National American Woman Suffrage Association, Carrie Chapman Catt, insists that women be rewarded for their war work by being granted the right to vote.
November 11, 1918	The signing of the Armistice ends the First World War. Americans, as a whole, begin feeling more optimistic and ready for more lighthearted moments.
1919	6.8 million cars are on the roads in the United States.
	Actors Charlie Chaplin, Douglas Fairbanks Sr., and Mary Pickford, along with director D. W. Griffith, form their own movie studio: United Artists.

January 16, 1919	Three-fourths of the states ratify legislation that leads to Prohibition.
October 28, 1919	Congress passes the Volstead Act, which defines illegal alcohol content and sets penalties for making, distributing, or selling alcoholic beverages.
1920	23.6% of the U.S. workforce is female, with 8.3 million females, ages 15 and up, working outside the home.
	For the first time in American history, more people live in cities (54.3 million) than rural areas (51.4 million).
	35 million people attend a movie each week.
	Congress establishes the U.S. Department of Labor Women's Bureau to protect the rights and needs of women earning wages.
January 1920	Prohibition goes into effect.
September 3, 1920	Silent film star Roscoe "Fatty" Arbuckle is accused of raping a starlet on this date.
August 26, 1920	Women officially earn the right to vote by the passage of the 19th Amendment.
November 2, 1920	Women can vote for the president of the United States for the first time.
	Westinghouse broadcasts the first-ever commercial radio programming, choosing this date so that they can report on the presidential election between Warren G. Harding and James M. Cox.
1921	Al Capone moves to Chicago to become the lieutenant for the ruthless John Torrio. After Torrio is shot and wounded by rival gang members, Capone takes over the Chicago criminal organization.

1924	Approximately 600 commercial radio stations exist, just four years after the first-ever commercial radio program was broadcast.
	Louise Brooks becomes a chorus girl in *George White's Scandals* and is the first woman to dance the Charleston in London.
	Charlie Chaplin releases the popular movie, *The Gold Rush*.
1925	Bessie Smith records a song, "Cake Walking Babies," using a microphone.
July 10, 1925	John Scopes is the center of a highly controversial trial after being charged with teaching evolution in a Dayton, Tennessee, school.
1926	*Vanity Fair* publishes an article about singer Bessie Smith, introducing large numbers of white Americans to the musical style known as the blues.
	Elinor Glyn writes *It*, first as a book and then a movie script; the term becomes part of jazz age slang.
April 1926	Editor H. L. Mencken publishes a true story by Herbert Asbury in the *American Mercury* about a prostitute. Accused of publishing obscene material, Mencken successfully fights the charges.
1927	57 million people attend a movie each week.
	The Bureau of Internal Revenue estimates that Capone generated $105 million in income during this year, although he did not claim that income.
April 30, 1927	The first two stars leave their prints in wet cement in front of Grauman's Chinese Theater: Mary Pickford and Douglas Fairbanks Sr.

May 21, 1927	Charles Lindbergh successfully flies solo across the Atlantic Ocean, the first person to ever do so.
October 6, 1927	Warner Bros. Pictures releases *The Jazz Singer* starring Al Jolson; this is the first full-length "talkie" movie.
1929	122 million cars are on the road in the United States.
	80 million people attend a movie each week.
February 14, 1929	In what becomes known as the bloody St. Valentine's Day Massacre, Al Capone's henchmen kill those of the rival gangster, George "Bugs" Moran.
May 16, 1929	The first Academy Awards are given out, with William Wellman's *Wings* chosen as best picture.
October 24, 1929	The stock market crashes, effectively ending the social and cultural conditions that had allowed the flapper lifestyle to flourish.

The Decade of the 1920s: The Flapper Era

Leading into the 1920s

The decade preceding the 1920s was tumultuous, filled with large-scale international tragedies, including the First World War in which an estimated 37,000,000 casualties (deaths and injuries) occurred worldwide, with about 117,000 Americans perishing and 204,000 suffering from sometimes debilitating wounds.[1] Moreover, as the bloody war was winding down, a deadly influenza epidemic arrived in three waves during 1918 and 1919 in the United States and around the world.

Between 20 and 40 million people died of this flu, which has been called history's most devastating epidemic to date. It killed more people in one year than the "Black Death" bubonic plague did between 1347 and 1351 combined.[2] No one was exempt from catching this disease, either; as President Woodrow Wilson negotiated the Versailles Treaty to end the war, he was suffering from this deadly flu.

From the Gibson Girl to the Flapper

When the 1920s dawned, both the war and the flu epidemic had ended and people desperately wanted this large-scale suffering to cease. Although the United States had participated in the war for fewer than two years, the armistice with Germany on November 11, 1918, brought a collective sigh of relief and a sense of optimism for the future, as the "war to end all wars" came to a close.

Although no single event or date is the watermark for the enormous social and cultural changes that were to take place during the 1920s, this decade was vastly different from the preceding one. Using the prevalent fashion for young women as a key benchmark of social change, this remarkable transition from the 1910s to the 1920s can be dramatically illustrated.

During most of the 1910s, the feminine ideal in the United States was the Gibson Girl, created by illustrator Charles Dana Gibson in the late nineteenth century. Gibson used his wife and her sisters as models for his sketches, which appeared in top magazines of the day, including *Harper's*, *Collier's Weekly*, and *Life*. The Gibson Girl, although slender, boasted a curvy, hourglass figure, thanks to a swan-bill corset beneath her bustled dress. Her neck was graceful, her hair piled upon her head with wisps and curls tumbling out, and her facial features were attractive and youthful, her beauty fresh-faced. The Gibson Girl was elegant yet approachable and charming, intelligent and capable without making demands of equality.

This style remained in fashion until the war began, at which time women began favoring more practical, shirtwaist-style dresses. These dresses appeared like a man's shirt in the bodice and sleeves, with a collar and buttons down the front. At the time, it would have seemed logical to assume that, postwar, the previous Gibson Girl style, which had defined fashion for about two decades, would return. That, however, did not happen. The flapper clothing that did come into style revolutionized women's fashion in the United States; the long skirt would never return as the primary fashion for women.

Instead, the dresses daringly inched up to calf length, then knee length; from 1926 through 1928, the knees themselves were exposed. When flappers danced the Charleston, a provocative dance perfected by the black community in Harlem and then performed by young women around the nation, they rouged those exposed knees. Flappers bound their breasts, in radical contrast to the Gibson Girl curves; bared their arms; neglected to cinch their waists; wore flashy stockings; and painted their faces with bright and bold cosmetics. Gabrielle

"Coco" Chanel was the clothing designer of choice for many of the females who could afford her work, and this style was copied by other less exclusive dress designers and manufacturers. Flappers' hair was often chopped to chin length, with a cloche hat frequently completing the look, and long strings of beads or pearls often worn as the untamed finishing touch.

This attention to fashion and frolic was fueled by a robust economy, although the early part of the decade was economically uncertain. After the war ended in November 1918, the federal government cut spending to a degree that matched 16 percent of the country's gross national product. The Federal Reserve reduced the money supply by 5.2 percent. So it's remarkable that the 1921 recession was as mild as what occurred.[3]

After the economy righted itself, the 1920s saw gross domestic product growth of 4.8 percent annually without the complications of inflation. Investors bought stocks by paying only 10 percent of their value, using the stocks themselves as collateral for the difference. By 1929 unemployment was low, just over 3 percent, as "real wages and corporate profits exploded; the stock market index grew by more than 23 percent per year during the 1920s, reaching an all-time high on September 3, 1929."[4]

Cultural Changes

America became more educated during the twenties, as attendance at larger universities doubled between 1915 and 1930. Because of the plethora of media, ranging from magazines such as the *New Yorker* and the *Saturday Evening Post*, and commercial radio broadcasting, which began in 1920, people had multiple opportunities to engage more fully in the world around them. Americans also became significantly more mobile, as car ownership skyrocketed from 6.8 million cars in 1919 to an astonishing 122 million in 1929.

Social values became less conservative as, for the first time in American history, more people lived in cities (54.3 million) than rural areas (51.4 million). City dwellers had significantly more opportunities to visit jazz clubs and speakeasies and women in cities were more likely to work outside the home, providing them with an independent income and broadening their life experiences. In 1920 Congress created the U.S. Department of Labor Women's Bureau to protect the rights and needs of women earning wages.

The growth of commercial radio programming, the effects of city dwelling, and the increasing numbers of women in the workplace are explored in greater depth in the chapter titled, "The First Modern Liberated Woman: The Flapper."

Women's Rights

Women earned the right to vote in 1920. Although they did not become a strong political force during the twenties, the 19th Amendment radically increased the power of women to effect change. The attention to child labor laws, as just one example, can be partially attributed to politicians' desires to tout family values to appeal to women's sensibilities. Also in the 1920s, a woman named Margaret Sanger tirelessly advocated for the acceptance of birth control; over time, its usage would dramatically provide females with more independence and control over their bodies.

Sanger's advocacy for birth control was occurring at the peak of the eugenics movement, which purported that the human population could reach its highest ideal through selective reproduction. This belief originated in 1883 with a British biologist named Francis Galton; by the 1920s, not only had it reached America, but it had become a mainstream belief. Simply put, eugenics stood for preventing the reproduction of weaker, less perfect humans and for the promotion of reproduction for the most morally fit humans; some but not all believers used this philosophy for racist purposes. Sanger piggybacked on the eugenics movement, pushing for the legitimization of birth control as a family planning tool. It is not surprising that Sanger would see the benefits of family planning, after watching her mother become increasingly exhausted after 18 pregnancies and 11 live births.

In 1921 Sanger organized America's first national birth-control conference; in 1925, she spearheaded the first international conference. She opened a birth-control clinic in New York City in 1923, which stayed open for about 50 years; that same year, she formed the National Committee on Federal Legislation for Birth Control. Before

Sanger's efforts, women purchased diaphragms in Bloomingdale's and contraceptive douches from Sears, in spite of a federal obscenity law that made sales of contraceptives illegal. The careful uses of euphemisms such as "feminine hygiene" products kept these methods of contraceptives available to women, but this was not enough for proponents of the birth-control movement of the 1920s, who advocated putting birth-control dispensation into the hands of physicians.[5]

Prohibition

Yet another constitutional amendment was added in this era: the 18th Amendment, which prohibited the manufacture, distribution, and sale of alcoholic beverages. Although it is impossible to know precisely how this affected the amount of alcohol consumed, speakeasies flourished throughout the country during the twenties, with men and women enjoying illicitly produced bathtub gin. The manufacturing, distributing, and selling of alcohol largely came under the control of gangsters such as Al Capone, who relied upon bribes and violence to establish power. The significance of Prohibition in American history and culture is great enough to have an entire chapter dedicated to it; see "Prohibition in the Flapper Era" below.

Arts

Music, theater, and literature flourished in the 1920s, as George and Ira Gershwin, Bessie Smith, Duke Ellington, and others created and performed extraordinary music. The twenties were the age of glamorous movie stars, ranging from flapper stars such as Louise Brooks, Olive Thomas, and Colleen Moore to the smoldering Rudolph Valentino and to the comic genius of Charlie Chaplin, Buster Keaton, and others. In 1927 Al Jolson starred in the first "talkie," a movie that contained dialogue as well as a soundtrack; the movie was *The Jazz Singer*. Writers of significant influence ranged from F. Scott Fitzgerald to Robert Benchley, Dorothy Parker, and more. The influence of the arts is explored in greater detail in the chapters "F. Scott and Zelda Fitzgerald: The Flapper Era Personified" and "From Silent to

Talkie: The World of Film," as well as in several of the biographies of key people from the 1920s.

Harlem Renaissance

A 1926 interview of Bessie Smith in *Vanity Fair* introduced a significant audience of white people to the musical style known as the blues. A new movement flowered in the same era: "The Harlem Renaissance, also known as the New Negro Movement, was a literary, artistic, cultural, intellectual movement that began in Harlem, New York after World War I and ended around 1935 during the Great Depression. The movement raised significant issues affecting the lives of African Americans through various forms of literature, art, music, drama, painting, sculpture, movies, and protests."[6] Poet Langston Hughes, in his autobiography *The Big Sea*, wrote about the 1920s: "It was the period when the Negro was in vogue." In this age of rebellion, it is not surprising that many whites flocked to see black singers in Harlem clubs and speakeasies, some owned by whites and catering to white audiences. Hughes labeled one of the most famous, the Cotton Club, as "a Jim Crow club for gangsters and monied whites."[7]

It also made sense that this cultural renaissance occurred in New York, which was one of the few states in the United States to prohibit racial segregation in schools; therefore, black students in New York had more opportunities to receive better schooling than in most other states. Moreover, New York was a center for the black movement overall. By 1930, the black population in Harlem was already 200,000 strong, with organizations such as the National Association for the Advancement of Colored People (NAACP) and the Urban League having been formed there.

The 1920s has also been called the decade of the "Great Migration," as blacks left southern states in increasing numbers, leaving behind the depressed agriculture economy in the South for the booming industrial opportunities in the northern states. Others left the South to become part of the protest movement gaining momentum in Harlem; W. E. B. Du Bois had been writing editorial pieces for the NAACP magazine, *Crisis*, which helped to fuel the protest movement. During this era, the black community believed that a success for any black person was a boon for the race overall.

Ku Klux Klan

Although positive momentum was taking place for blacks in the cultural arts and entertainment fields, a negative force was gaining strength as well. The 1920s brought a resurgence of the Ku Klux Klan (KKK). The KKK originally formed shortly after the Civil War ended in 1865 to control and intimidate former slaves. It was supported by former Confederates who used burning crosses, often placed on the front lawns of blacks or on the lawns of those who supported and/or protected them, as a trademark form of intimidation. Although its influence died down as Reconstruction was completed, the organization regained power during the twenties. KKK members promoted themselves as "true" Americans who protected traditional beliefs and morals, as they engaged in campaigns of hate towards blacks, Jewish and Catholic people, and immigrants.

The KKK revival first sparked in 1915 when *Birth of a Nation*, an epic film directed by D. W. Griffith, appeared on screens nationwide, lauding KKK members as heroes. The organization gained further momentum in 1920 when Edward Clarke, a former journalist, and Bessie Tyler, a former madam, oversaw an organization originally formed to raise funds for some First World War initiatives, transforming it into the Southern Publicity Association, and bolstering membership from 3,000 to three million. Each time that a new member joined, Clarke and Tyler donated part of the $10 fee to the Klan. The KKK gained power in another way as well, helping to get 16 men elected as senators, as well as a number of state representatives and local politicians. In 1924 the Klan claimed to have control over 50 percent of the state legislatures; that same year, the people of Kansas voted in a governor who was associated with the Klan. Throughout the twenties, the Klan's influence was significant, with as many as eight million people belonging to the KKK during the organization's peak.

It might be expected that Klan members were themselves marginalized in society; in fact, a significant percentage of its members were middle-class and above, with doctors, lawyers, and even ministers joining. It is also sometimes assumed that the Klan only operated in the southern states, especially since its headquarters were in Atlanta, Georgia. Although southern states did serve as the organization's stronghold overall, at one time there were 300,000 members in Ohio alone, with 200,000 in Pennsylvania.[8] Other areas of strength included Oklahoma, New Jersey, New York, Kansas, Colorado, Montana, California, Oregon, Michigan, and Indiana. Author Leonard Moore stated that the Klan in fact reached its highest levels of infiltration in Indiana. Although some members hid their activities, others proudly marched in parades and openly campaigned for political candidates endorsed by the KKK. According to Moore, "The popularity of this ideology, historians have generally concluded, could be traced to a sense of national peril, a pervasive fear by native white Protestants that rural, small-town culture had lost its place at the center of American life, that the nation had been delivered into the hands of urbanites, anarchists, and immigrants."[9]

Baseball and Disillusionment

Although overall the twenties were a time of hope and optimism, countless thousands of baseball fans were disillusioned by what became known as the Black Sox Scandal. Although the impetus for the scandal occurred in 1919, it exploded into national consciousness in 1920–1921. The 1919 World Series was played between the favored Chicago White Sox of the American League—with star "Shoeless" Joe Jackson in the lineup—and the Cincinnati Reds of the National League. Baseball fans from coast to coast were shocked when the Sox lost the Series to the Reds; rumblings of thrown games were heard during the Series and eventually these rumors were printed in the newspapers.

Ultimately, eight members of the White Sox team—labeled the "Black Sox"—were accused of conspiring with gamblers to deliberately lose the Series in exchange for a cash payoff; the gamblers, the accusations went, benefited by betting on the Reds, while the Black Sox were paid for their cooperation. These players were indicted on charges of fraud; although not convicted, they were banned from baseball for life—and fans of the era felt cheated and disenchanted with professional baseball. Had it not been for a player of extraordinary talent—George Herman "Babe" Ruth—it's unlikely that professional baseball would have so quickly recovered. Four times that decade, Ruth hit more than 50 home runs a season, including one where he hit 60; this was the single-season home-run record until 1961. During the 1920s, he hit a total of 467 home runs, a record that still stands today.

Conclusion

The 1920s, like every other decade before and since, contained a combination of positive forces and negative ones. The Jazz Age, however, boasted more dramatic ups and downs than typical, including two constitutional amendments; sweeping social change, especially for young women; the influence of gangsters such as Al Capone; perhaps the biggest baseball scandal to date; the tipping point that changed the United States from a more rural nation to a more urban one; the growth of the contributions of black Americans to our national culture and the re-emergence of the KKK; the plethora of automobiles and the growth of airplane travel; and much more. The amount of music, literature, and film created was astonishing and, in many instances, these creative works were extraordinary. At the peak of ebullient pleasure enjoyed by the youth of the era, surely it must have seemed as though these good times would never end; the decade associated with the age of the flappers did end, however, and in a dramatic fashion that seems appropriate, given the spectacular ways in which American culture changed during the twenties.

The Roaring Twenties and the age of the flappers effectively ended when the stock market crashed on Thursday, October 24, 1929, then continued its catastrophic collapse on the following Monday and Tuesday. The wild pursuit of hedonism came to a screeching halt for many who nearly instantaneously lost their personal wealth and security, as the country declined into a deep and long-lasting economic depression. Although the lifestyle of the flapper died even more rapidly than it was birthed, the influence of this era lives on, especially in the lives of women who gained significantly more freedoms during this controversial whirlwind decade.

Notes

1. Historians debate the accuracy of data about casualties; different sources list different figures.
2. "The Influenza Pandemic of 1918," Stanford University, http://virus.stanford.edu/uda, modified February 2005 (accessed May 21, 2009).
3. "The Rising Risk of Recession," *Time*, December, 19, 1969, http://www.time.com/time/magazine/article/0,9171,941750-5,00.html (accessed May 21, 2009).
4. John L. Chapman, "Fighting Recession with Panic," *The American*, March 18, 2008, http://www.american.com/archive/2008/march-03-08/fighting-recession-with-panic (accessed May 21, 2009).
5. Amy Sarch, "Dirty Discourse: Birth Control Advertising in the 1920s and 1930s," University of Pennsylvania—Electronic Dissertations, Paper AAI9427611, January 1, 1994, http://repository.upenn.edu/dissertations/AAI9427611 (accessed May 21, 2009).
6. "Harlem Renaissance," John Carroll University, http://www.jcu.edu/harlem (accessed May 21, 2009).
7. Langston Hughes, *The Big Sea* (New York: Hill and Wang, 1940); Caroline Jackson, "Harlem Renaissance: Pivotal Period in the Development of Afro-American Culture," *Yale–New Haven Teachers Institute* 2 (1978), http://www.yale.edu/ynhti/curriculum/units/1978/2/78.02.03.x.html (accessed May 21, 2009).
8. "People and Events: The Rise of the Ku Klux Klan in the 1920s," *American Experience*, PBS, http://www.pbs.org/wgbh/amex/flood/peopleevents/e_klan.html (accessed May 21, 2009).
9. Leonard J. Moore, *Citizen Klansmen: The Ku Klux Klan in Indiana, 1921–1928* (Chapel Hill: University of North Carolina Press, 1991), 3.

CHAPTER TWO

The First Modern Liberated Woman: The Flapper

No one knows precisely how the term "flapper" came to represent what it did, which was the ultramodern and audacious young woman who danced and drank; smoked chic cigarettes; bobbed her hair and showed her shins; and shook and shimmied in jazz halls and clubs of uncertain reputation. One writer of the 1920s believed this designation evolved from the sleek "flapper dresses" that young women considered fashionable and that differed significantly from the modest ankle-length frocks worn by their mothers' generation.

However the term "flapper" originated, negative connotations quickly attached themselves to it, with the Florida state legislature even considering banning the word itself. It is ironic, then, that as politicians attempted to remove their label from the mainstay of language, flappers were busy crafting their own creative slang, with numerous quirky phrases conveying information about their rebellious activities. If, for example, a perky flapper shared that she was about to "see a man about a dog," she was really on her way to buy whiskey made illegal by the Volstead Act, better known as Prohibition. If flappers giggled about "barney-mugging," illicit sex was also part of the scene. The upbeat nature of most flappers was also reflected in their slang, with phrases such as "the bee's knees," "the cat's pajamas," and "That's so Jake" all representing something marvelous.

Although it isn't unusual for clashes to occur between generations, they seemed especially intense during this era. Mothers, who had always worn long skirts corseted to emphasize their womanly hourglass curves, and who had pulled their long hair up into pompadour styles, wondered how they had gone so terribly wrong in guiding their daughters. Perhaps these same mothers, many of whom had fought hard to abolish alcoholic drink—and who had briefly tasted success when the Volstead Act passed—now struggled to understand why their beautiful girls drank bathtub gin as they frequented speakeasies.

What happened? How did such a significant cultural change take place? And how did these changes help this generation of young women to become more independent and more liberated than any other previous generation of females in the history of the United States? Finally, how do their liberated lifestyles compare to those of twenty-first-century women?

Ending of War

When the armistice was signed with Germany in November 1918 and the brutal war officially ended, people in the United States were weary of suffering and sacrifice and ready to embrace life with a renewed sense of optimism and hope, and to experience moments of lightness and gaiety. To quote a history of the 1920s titled *Dancing Fools and Weary Blues: The Great Escape of the Twenties*: "Whether there was freedom and a new chance for all—and there was not— there existed an erroneous but cheering belief that there was change ahead. The openness of the future and the accessibility, as it seemed, of success produced a froth upon the surface of society."[1]

Although the United States participated in the war for a relatively short time, from April 6, 1917, through its ending in November 1918, American culture changed significantly during that window of time. With more than four million American males mobilized for the war effort, women entered the workforce in ever increasing numbers, working in offices and factories, in stores and governmental agencies, and more. Women also served in the Red Cross and participated in other humanitarian efforts. Overall, they were earning higher wages than they ever had in the past; some of these women—whether they had worked outside the home before or not—found themselves working in previously male-dominated fields.

These changes gave women an increased sense of self-confidence and independence and it is not surprising that they did not want the previous social structure to return. Actress Colleen Moore identified with these sentiments, saying, "I shared their restlessness, understood their determination to free themselves of the Victorian shackles of the pre–World War I era and find out for themselves what life was all about."[2] By 1920, nearly one-fourth of the workforce (23.6 percent) was female, with 8.3 million females, aged 15 and up, working outside the home.

Right to Vote

While the war gave women new opportunities and raised both their economic status and sense of independence, an additional opportunity of huge significance was legislated at the beginning of the twenties decade: the right to vote. Suffragists had been fighting for the woman's vote since July 1848, when Elizabeth Cady Stanton and Lucretia Mott organized the Seneca Falls Women's Rights Convention in New York. In 1878 a suffrage amendment was introduced in Congress, although it did not receive enough votes for its passage for more than 40 years.

In 1918 the head of the National American Woman Suffrage Association, Carrie Chapman Catt, insisted that women be rewarded for their war work by receiving the right to vote, contacting both President Woodrow Wilson and members of Congress. That September, Wilson responding by saying, "We have made partners of the women in this war. Shall we admit them only to a partnership of suffering and sacrifice and toil and not to a partnership of right?"

By this point, political momentum was in favor of female suffrage and in August 1920, after a struggle of many decades, women finally earned the right to vote in the United States through the 19th Amendment to the Constitution. This text, unchanged since its creation in 1878, reads, "The right of citizens of the United States to vote shall not be denied or abridged by the United States or by any State on account of sex. Congress shall have power to enforce this article by appropriate legislation." Because of this amendment, in all but two states—Georgia and Mississippi—women could vote in the 1920 presidential election between Warren G. Harding and James M. Cox. Georgia and Mississippi both had a statute that required voter registration at least four months prior to an election, which prevented women in those states from voting in 1920.

Overall, approximately one in three eligible female voters took advantage of their new privilege in 1920; according to an article in the *New York Times*, "On the whole women liked the vote and men liked to have them vote. The timid who ventured into politics with many reservations found the casting of a vote easier and more interesting than they had supposed."[3]

It was during this decade that the National Woman's Party proposed an Equal Rights Amendment to eliminate discrimination based on gender, an amendment that to date has not been passed by Congress.

Members of the National Woman's Party, including chairperson Alice Paul, seek support in June 1920 for the ratification of the 19th Amendment granting women the right to vote. (AP Photo.)

Urban versus Rural Living

Prior to the 1920s more Americans lived on farms and in small towns than in cities. In the year 1920, though, more people lived in cities than towns for the first time in the history of the United States (54.3 million urban versus 51.4 million rural).[4] Plus, the change was more radical than just a shift in percentages. According to "Clash of Cultures: America in the 1920s," a research paper made available by the Newton Public School System, "The farmer, who had occupied a favored place in American mythology since the time of Thomas Jefferson, rapidly gave way to the industrialist, the capitalist, and the Entrepreneur." Statistics bear out this observation; in the 1920s, for every 46 people involved in farming, there were 54 in manufacturing/mechanical industries, with the gross national product (GNP) of manufactured products being three times that of agricultural production.

As people began moving to cities in increasing numbers, their lifestyles changed. Cities have more theaters and nightclubs and other venues where more daring activities—smoking, drinking, dancing, and so forth—are likely to occur. Women, rather than working at home on the family farm, were more likely to get jobs in restaurants, offices, factories, and other locations that took them away from home. All of these factors, when added together, created an environment wherein females had more freedom—and income—than in the past.

Prior to this time, as author George E. Mowry points out, the "country's social goals and aspirations had been traditionally set by small groups of preachers, politicians, lawyers, editors, and teachers, and later as well by the economic elite spawned by post-Civil War industrialism."[5] The 1920s, though, with its shift to urban living, saw the tastes of the masses pushed to the forefront, making the twenties the decade that witnessed the birth of popular (pop) culture.

Manufacturing and Technology

As the United States was becoming increasingly urban, technology was advancing at faster speeds and mass production was becoming a way of life. In fact, industrial production increased by 60 percent during this decade, outstripping population growth, which was closer to 15 percent.

In order for mass production to become financial profitable and therefore sustainable, there must also be mass consumption—which meant that for the first time in history it was key for manufacturers, wholesalers, and retailers to appeal to the tastes of large demographic groups. Not surprisingly, advertising hit new strides in this era, tempting people with discretionary income to purchase the latest of fashions and the sleekest new automobiles, and to spend freely at nightclubs and restaurants and theaters.

Mass production also allowed the working class women to dress in facsimiles of what only the rich would have otherwise worn, and these more affordable fashions allowed these women to change their personal styles as trends dictated.

Leisure Time

As factories continued to produce material goods, technology stream-lined the labor needed to create these goods, which meant that leisure time was also increasing; the average work week scaled back from 60 hours to 48. Plus, middle-class and working-class families were more likely to have vacuum cleaners, refrigerators, and other household appliances that lightened the labor needed to maintain a home. Shoppers could buy already baked bread, canned soups, frozen vegetables, peanut butter, breakfast cereals, and other foods that required little preparation, which also added to their leisure time.

As leisure time increased, so did access to leisure activities, whether that meant listening to the radio, watching silent—and then talking—movies, dancing at smoky jazz clubs, or taking thrilling Sunday afternoon drives. This was also the era of fads such as marathon dancing, roller derby races, or flag-pole sitting; in earlier eras, most men and women would not have had enough time to participate in such activities.

Transportation

Although Henry Ford had begun manufacturing automobiles via an assembly line in 1913, people did not necessarily purchase one during

Cutting-edge Dior fashion as of February 16, 1929. (AP Photo.)

the war years. After the war ended, though, automobile purchases started to increase; in 1919 the United States had approximately 6.8 million cars and a population of 105 million. Car ownership nearly quadrupled during the 1920s, with 23 million cars on the road by 1929, when the population was 122 million.

Automobiles boosted the opportunities for travel along with the opportunities for young adults to socialize outside the home, away from the watchful eyes of parents, relatives, and neighbors. Visiting jazz clubs, traveling from one party to the next, and slipping into speakeasies all became immeasurably easier with an automobile; this also increased the likelihood that a woman could have transportation to a job. The fact that consumers could purchase a car on credit (with more than half of the automobiles of the era being bought this way) meant that people with lower wages could also own a vehicle.

Parents and preachers, community leaders and teachers spoke out against unchaperoned females riding in automobiles with males, with one college dean calling the automobile "one of the prime causes of the 'riotous license'" of the era.[6] "Petting parties," which often took place in the back seats of cars, were loudly denounced, often to no avail.

Meanwhile, airplanes gradually became an integral part of American society. During the war, the government invested heavily in aero-technology and, by the end of the 1920s, cities of significant size had airports and regularly scheduled flights. On May 21, 1927, Charles Lindbergh successfully completed the first trans-Atlantic flight. Although a typical flapper might not fly across the country, the mind-set of the country was expanding as its horizons were.

Movies

The effect of the movies on the culture of the day cannot be emphasized enough. In 1920, 35 million Americans—one out of three—went to the movies every single week. When the "talkies" were introduced in 1927, that number skyrocketed to 57 million each week. By the end of the decade, Americans were buying 80 million tickets every week, which meant that more than one out of every two people attended the movies on a weekly basis.[7]

Movies gave middle-class and working-class youth a glimpse of the exciting lives of the rich and the famous—or at least Hollywood's version of this luxurious lifestyle. According to Mowry, "A chicken in every pot, a car in every garage, film star beauty for every adolescent girl, and perhaps an adultery for every marriage—these were the promises and the expectations of the Twenties."[8]

When young women went to the movies, what did they see and how did it influence them? Prior to the war, female protagonists tended to be innocent and ladylike, needing the men in their families to protect them. After the war, the women in films were more independent and self-assured, dressed in more daring, slinky clothing, and often engaged in activities previously considered appropriate only for men: drinking, smoking, and dancing. Surely these women served as role models for millions of moviegoers.

Radio

Although the technology for radios had existed since 1907, there weren't any practical applications of the radio at that time, and so this device was mostly used by ham-radio fanatics who communicated only with one another. In 1920, though, radio manufacturer Westinghouse decided to offer radio programming to increase interest in the device. Programming began on November 2, 1920, when Pittsburgh's KDKA broadcast information about the presidential election occurring that day between Harding and Cox.

After Westinghouse's stroke of genius, people began purchasing radios in droves. Between 1923 and 1930, 60 percent of families in the United States owned radios. By 1924, 600 commercial stations were operating; to make the stations financially viable, station staff began to sell advertising—which added to the culture of mass consumption. Headsets, a vital part of early radios, were replaced with speakers, which allowed groups of people to listen to the radio together and experience mass communication, which fed into the creation of pop culture in the twenties.

The Liberated Woman

So, how liberated were the women of the twenties? When compared to the Victorian upbringing of their mothers and grandmothers, they were quite liberated—or at least a significant portion of them were—for all of the reasons just named.

Compared to twenty-first-century women of the same age, though, they do not seem as free. Stipulating that one definition of liberation is having more options available, marriage data would indicate that today's women are significantly more liberated than those from the 1920s. In the 1920s, the crude marriage rate was 99 out of every 1,000 single women, while the rate in 1988 was only 76 out of 1,000. By 2004, the crude marriage rate was only 39.9 per 1,000. Research and census data indicate that more twenty-first-century women are choosing to cohabit rather than marry, with 41 percent of women in 2000 having cohabited with a male. Although some family reformers in the 1920s advocated brief cohabitation as a "trial marriage," cohabitation was not considered socially acceptable in the twenties.[9]

The fact that 23.6 percent of women in 1920 worked outside the home was an indicator that women were gaining economic power; yet, those figures pale in comparison to modern-day figures. By 2007, for example, 46 percent of the U.S. labor force was female and, by 2016, the projected figure is 47 percent. Perhaps even more important, in 2007, 51 percent of people in high-paying management/professional occupations were female.[10]

In 1920 Congress established the U.S. Department of Labor Women's Bureau to protect the rights and needs of women earning wages. It was not until 1963, though, that Congress passed the Equal Pay Act to ensure that men and women performing the same jobs received the same pay; this issue has still not been fully addressed, although progress has clearly been made.

Advertisements were targeting women in the 1920s, which indicates that companies recognized that women did have buying power. However, the messages in the ads usually reflected more traditional thinking. For example, one 1920s ad for Pond's cold cream featured Alva Belmont from the National Woman's Party; her message was "A woman who neglects her personal appearance loses half her influence." Another advertisement, this one for Marie Barlow Cosmetics in *Vogue* magazine, has this text: "For men demand youth in women's faces!" Yet another advertisement reads: "You think I'm a flapper but I can keep house." Overall, the ads stressed domesticity and pleasing men over any messages of independence.

These are just a few of the multiple benchmarks that can be used to see how the women of the flapper era had begun to gain independence and liberation, as well as the ways in which traditional roles and beliefs from the Victorian age still held sway when compared to the lifestyles of twenty-first-century women. Overall, it is fair to say that many women of the twenties enjoyed significantly more freedoms and independence than females of previous generations, with these advances serving as stepping stones for future generations of women.

Notes

1. Elizabeth Stevenson, "Flappers and Some Who Were Not Flappers," in *Dancing Fools and Weary Blues: The Great Escape of the Twenties*, ed. Lawrence R. Broer and John D. Walther (Bowling Green, OH: Bowling Green State University Popular Press, 1990), 122.

2. Liesl Schillinger, "The Beautiful and Damned," review of *Flapper: A Madcap Story of Sex, Style, Celebrity, and the Women Who Made America Modern* by Joshua Zeitz, *New York Times*, April 16, 2006, http://www.nytimes.com/2006/04/16/books/review/16schilinger.html?_r=1&scp=1&sq=zeitz%2C+flapper&st=nyt (accessed April 7, 2009).

3. William L. Chenery, "One in Three Women Vote," *New York Times*, December 19, 1920, http://query.nytimes.com/mem/archive-free/pdf?res=990DEED9103FE432A2575AC1A9649D946195D6CF (accessed April 5, 2009).

4. Amos St. Germain, "The Flowering of Mass Society: An Historical Overview of the 1920s," in *Dancing Fools and Weary Blues*, ed. Broer and Walther, 26.

5. George Mowry, ed., *The Twenties: Fords, Flappers, and Fanatics* (Englewood Cliffs, NJ: Prentice-Hall, 1963), 1.

6. Helen Bullitt Lowry, "Mrs. Grundy on the Job of Reforming the Flapper," *New York Times*, March 27, 1921, 15, http://query.nytimes.com/mem/archivefree/pdf?_r=1&res=9F02EFD8113FE432A25754C2A9659C946095D6CF (accessed April 7, 2009).

7. Patricia Erens, "The Flapper: Hollywood's First Liberated Woman," in *Dancing Fools and Weary Blues*, ed. Broer and Walther, 131.

8. Mowry, ed., *The Twenties*, 43.

9. Patricia H. Shiono and Linda Sandham Quinn, "Epidemiology of Divorce," *The Future of Children* 4, no. 1 (Spring/Summer 1994), http://www.futureofchildren.org/information2827/information_show.htm?doc_id=75526 (accessed April 7, 2009); Barbara Dafoe Whitehead and David Popenoe, "Essay: Marriage and Family: What Does the Scandinavian Experience Tell Us?" *The State of Our Unions: The Social Health of Marriage in America*, The National Marriage Project, 2005, http://marriage.rutgers.edu/Publications/SOOU/TEXTSOOU2005.htm (accessed April 7, 2009); Alternatives to Marriage Project, http://www.unmarried.org/statistics.html (accessed April 7, 2009); Ben Wattenberg, "Cohabitating Couples," *The First Measured Century*, PBS, http://www.pbs.org/fmc/book/4family3.htm (accessed April 7, 2009).

10. U.S. Department of Labor, Women's Bureau, http://www.dol.gov/wb/stats/main.htm (accessed April 7, 2009).

CHAPTER THREE

F. Scott and Zelda Fitzgerald: The Flapper Era Personified

Perhaps no other couple personified the frantic hedonism of the flapper era more than Francis Scott Key Fitzgerald and Zelda Sayre Fitzgerald. F. Scott Fitzgerald, who was a distant relative of the man who wrote the "Star Spangled Banner," penned numerous novels and short stories that captured the glittering youth culture of the twenties and highlighted the lifestyle of the independent flapper. What Fitzgerald developed was the "ability not only to document the manners and mores, the fashions and fads of his times, but also to evaluate them—and himself—objectively."[1] Meanwhile, he and his wife danced and drank and loved and fought. Their lives were complicated by Fitzgerald's alcoholism, their financial ups and downs, Zelda's mental illness, and their love affairs.

Fitzgerald's interest in writing surfaced early in life, with his first story—a detective tale—appearing in a prep school newspaper when he was 13 years old. By 1917 he was writing scripts and song lyrics for the Princeton Triangle Club musicals, plus material for the *Princeton Tiger* humor magazine and the *Nassau Literary Magazine*. In 1924 Fitzgerald looked back at his collegiate experience, noting that he had failed freshman algebra, trigonometry, coordinate geometry, and hygiene, but that through summer tutoring he was able to return his sophomore year to act in an operetta that he had written for the Triangle Club.

Fitzgerald was on probation during much of his collegiate experience. Never graduating, he joined the army after acknowledging that he was not to find success in academics. Before leaving to report for military duty, he quickly wrote a novel, *The Romantic Egoist*; he wanted to finish a novel before potentially dying in war. He submitted the manuscript to Charles Scribner's Sons and received a rejection letter that encouraged Fitzgerald to revise the manuscript and then resubmit. Although he followed through, the revised manuscript was also rejected.

Fitzgerald's fears of dying in battle never came to fruition, as the war ended shortly before he was to go to Europe. In June 1918, while living at Camp Sheridan near Montgomery, Alabama, he met Zelda Sayre and romance ignited. Fitzgerald saw in Zelda the embodiment of the new modern woman. Described by one writer as "sensuous and impulsive," at 18 she was "accustomed to the limelight and even courted center stage with antics such as pinning mistletoe to the back of her skirt as if to challenge men to an inappropriate kiss."[2] Although Zelda was pursued by many men, she chose to become engaged to Fitzgerald.

Fitzgerald headed to New York and began working at an advertising firm, hoping to save enough money to marry and support Zelda. After she broke off their engagement, unsatisfied with Fitzgerald's ability to earn sufficient income, he quit his job and returned home to St. Paul, Minnesota, where he began revising his novel.[3] Renamed *This Side of Paradise*, the novel was accepted by Maxwell Perkins at Scribner's on September 16, 1919. Fitzgerald began writing numerous short stories, many of which were published in the *Saturday Evening Post*, the *Smart Set*, and *Scribner's Magazine*. Independent women appeared as characters in many of his early works, including "The Offshore Pirate" and "Bernice Bobs Her Hair."

This Side of Paradise was an instant success, selling out its first printing in just 24 hours. Significantly autobiographical, this novel shares the life of the idealistic Amory Blaine, a wealthy, pampered boy who attends prep school and then Princeton University. Blaine believes himself to have a great destiny in store, but he encounters numerous disappointments. In college, he becomes associated with the Triangle Club musicals, but then is ejected from college. He becomes disillusioned when a romance falters; like Fitzgerald, Blaine becomes a second lieutenant in the war. Afterwards, Blaine secures and then quits an advertising job. These are only some of the similarities between the plot of the novel and the life of F. Scott Fitzgerald. Although some critics pointed out the lack of discipline and control of Fitzgerald's writing, *This Side of Paradise* was praised for its originality and sophistication.

Just one week after its publication on March 26, 1920, Zelda changed her mind about Fitzgerald and they married on April 3. They immediately began living an extravagant lifestyle and became well known for their outrageous antics, which included jumping into the fountain at New York City's Union Square and being kicked out of hotels for drunkenly disturbing the other guests. Fitzgerald was earning significant amounts of money for his writing, $4,000 for one short story alone. In 1924 he wrote a tongue-in-cheek article, "How to Live on $36,000 a Year," using a figure more than 20 times what the average American earned. The Fitzgeralds, though, spent the money as quickly as it arrived, forcing Fitzgerald to pull his attention away from the artistic novels that he wanted to write to focus on slick stories for magazines that brought in quick cash.

Fitzgerald released his first collection of short stories in 1920, titled *Flappers and Philosophers*. A *New York Times* review, published on September 26, 1920, noted his "brilliance": "Not the most superficial reader can fail to recognize Mr. Fitzgerald's talent and genius."[4]

The couple toured Europe before returning to Minnesota, where their daughter, Frances Scott Fitzgerald, was born in October 1921. She was nicknamed "Scottie," a nickname that endured her entire life.

Fitzgerald followed up his first novel with the 1922 release of *The Beautiful and the Damned*, which was also somewhat autobiographical. In *The Beautiful and the Damned*, a young man named Anthony Patch awaits an inheritance from his wealthy grandfather. In his one moment of proactive behavior as he waits for his bequest, Patch woos and then marries the beautiful Gloria Gilbert and the two of them anticipate a life of riches and leisure. They overindulge in alcoholic drink, though, and soon the couple is at odds with one another. They struggle from financial woes, too, as Patch seldom works and the marriage continues to disintegrate. After they discover that they have in

Author Francis Scott Key Fitzgerald poses with his wife, Zelda, and daughter, Scottie, on July 16, 1925. (AP Photo.)

fact been disinherited, Anthony is drafted to fight in the war. While overseas, he has an affair and is reduced in rank over his behavior. Meanwhile, Gloria screen tests for a movie role and receives the disheartening news that, rather than being offered the part of the young beauty, her fading looks cause her to be offered the role of the rich widow. When Patch returns from the war, they fight to get the inheritance they feel they deserve; by the time the money is awarded to them, Patch is in a wheelchair and Gloria is a shadow of her former vital self.

Overall, *The Beautiful and the Damned* met with praise from critics, although the *New York Times* stated that "Not one of the book's many characters, important or unimportant, ever rises to the level of ordinary decent humanity. Not one of them shows a spark of loyalty, of honor, of devotion, of generosity, of real friendship or of real affection."[5] After the release of his second novel, Fitzgerald published a second collection of short stories, *Tales of the Jazz Age*; the October 29, 1922, *New York Times* review notes, "Indeed, if ever a writer was born with a gold pen in his mouth, surely Fitzgerald is that man. The more you read him, the more he convinces you that here is the destined artist."[6]

Fitzgerald had always been drawn to theatrical productions and the couple enjoyed attending plays, so he crafted a script, *The Vegetable: From President to Postman*. The protagonist in this play is a disgruntled clerk who dreams of becoming a postman. After awakening one day from a drunken slumber, he discovers that he has become the Republican candidate for the president of the United States. When he ends up in the White House, he endures nightmarish situations that turn out in fact to be nightmares. Opening on November 10, 1923, the play closed within one week, to Fitzgerald's horror and shame.

In 1924 the Fitzgeralds traveled to France, where Fitzgerald intended to focus on his next novel. Zelda's affair with a French aviator, however, caused the family to uproot once again, this time settling in Italy. On April 10, 1925, Fitzgerald published the book that most firmly established his literary legacy, *The Great Gatsby*.

The Great Gatsby is told in retrospect from the perspective of a secondary character, Nick Carraway, who visits his cousin, Daisy Buchanan, and her husband, Tom. They live in luxury, in contrast to Nick's more modest lifestyle. Across the body of water lives a mysterious man, Jay Gatsby, whom Nick once knew.

Complications arise. Nick and Tom visit Tom's mistress, Myrtle Wilson, at a drunken party. Tom breaks Myrtle's nose after they argue about Daisy, but their illicit relationship continues. Nick and Gatsby build a friendship over the summer, although much is still not known about Gatsby. What is learned is that Gatsby loves Daisy, a woman that he had met while a poor soldier. In the intervening years, he had gained immense wealth, all to impress Daisy and win her heart. Gatsby deliberately bought the house across the pond from Daisy and Tom for that purpose and Gatsby and Daisy are brought together again by Nick; when Tom and Daisy attend one of Gatsby's parties, Tom is too busy chasing other women to pay much attention to Daisy and Gatsby's time together.

Later that summer, Tom catches on to Daisy and Gatsby's affair on the same day that his mistress's husband determines that Myrtle is having an affair. Although the husband doesn't know with whom, he plans to take Myrtle elsewhere in the country to break up her relationship. So Tom effectively loses both his wife and mistress in one day.

After a day of heavy drinking with Gatsby and his wife and others, Tom begins asking Gatsby about his intentions with Daisy. Gatsby announces that he wants Daisy to admit that she has never loved Tom and has always loved Gatsby. Daisy won't do that, but Gatsby tells Tom that his wife will leave him for Gatsby; Tom, secure in the knowledge that his multigenerations-long family wealth and prestige is far more impressive than Gatsby's new wealth, knows that Daisy won't leave him. They all then head to Gatsby's house, with Gatsby and Daisy in one car, and the rest in the other.

When Tom drives by Myrtle's husband's garage, they discover that Myrtle has just been killed by a car—and the car did not stop. Even worse, it was Gatsby's car. Nick discovers that Daisy had been driving the car, but Gatsby plans to take the blame. Shortly thereafter, Myrtle's husband goes to Gatsby's house, shooting and killing him because he blames him for Myrtle's death; Myrtle's distraught husband then commits suicide.

Nick handles Gatsby's funeral, which is poorly attended; neither Daisy nor Tom is there. Nick then discovers that Tom had told Myrtle's husband that Gatsby was to blame for the hit-and-run. Nick, thoroughly disgusted with Tom and Daisy and their careless, heartless lifestyle, leaves his cousin's home.

Although this novel came out to critical acclaim, Fitzgerald did not earn much in royalties from its publication and he needed to return to writing short stories as a way to earn more cash. It was at this time that he developed a friendship with Ernest Hemingway. Fitzgerald considered Hemingway the epitome of literary artistry and he aspired to reach that pinnacle. Hemingway admired Fitzgerald's talent and creativity, but felt that his challenges with alcohol were self-destructive and a sign of moral weakness. Fitzgerald was deeply wounded when Hemingway used Fitzgerald as the subject of satire, making him an alcoholic clown in his novel, *The Torrents of Spring* (1926).

Other than the release of a collection of short stories, *All the Sad Young Men*, in 1926, Fitzgerald did not publish any more books until 1934. The Fitzgeralds lived abroad until the end of 1931, largely because it was less expensive. They fought often, fueled by the consumption of too much alcohol, Zelda's infidelity, and Fitzgerald's jealousy. Zelda, wanting her own opportunity to express herself artistically, intensely began studying dance.

During this time abroad, the Fitzgeralds endured a new challenge. After a 1929 return to France, Zelda's behavior became increasingly odd and, in April 1930, she was committed to a psychiatric clinic in Switzerland, where she was treated for schizophrenia and where she remained until September 1931. Fitzgerald paid for her treatment by writing more short stories. When they returned to the United States, Fitzgerald was commissioned to write a screenplay of *Red-Headed Woman* for Metro-Goldwyn-Mayer (MGM). His script, however, was rejected and, after Fitzgerald's drunken behavior at a party at director Irving Thalberg's house, the offer was rescinded.

Zelda relapsed in February 1932 and was treated at Johns Hopkins Hospital in Baltimore. For the rest of her life, she was either hospitalized or being treated as an outpatient. Fitzgerald continued to write short stories, some of which were his best work, to pay for her expensive treatment. While in Johns Hopkins, Zelda wrote a novel, *Save Me the Waltz*; her husband resented that she used material that he had intended for his next novel, *Tender Is the Night*, which was published on April 12, 1934.[7] This novel focused on a self-destructive relationship much like that of the Fitzgeralds. Unfortunately, people were not interested in reading about the upper-class couple featured in this novel when so many Americans were suffering through economically disastrous times; so, despite how well it was written, the novel was not a success.

Fitzgerald published his last book, a fourth collection of stories, on March 20, 1935: *Taps at Reveille*. By this time, Fitzgerald was suffering from tuberculosis and advanced alcoholism; twice he had attempted suicide. He published a series of essays in *Esquire* that shared how low he had sunk.

When their daughter turned 14, Fitzgerald sent her to a boarding school; after that, she never lived at home with him again. Meanwhile, Zelda was committed to Highland Hospital, where she remained for the rest of her life. The combined expenses of Scottie's schooling and Zelda's medical treatments plunged Fitzgerald even more deeply into debt.

In the summer of 1937 Fitzgerald received a contract from MGM, where he earned $1,000 a week for six months. Although he worked on multiple scripts, including *A Yank at Oxford*, *The Women*, and *Madame Curie*, as well as assisting with *Gone with the Wind*, this experience was not successful and it marked the end of his career in Hollywood.

After that contract ended, he focused on writing short stories and began another novel, *The Last Tycoon*. When that novel was about half done, he died of a heart attack in the apartment of his lover, Sheilah Graham, on December 21, 1940. Because he no longer observed the tenets of the Catholic Church, he was denied a Catholic funeral and not buried in his family's cemetery. Obituaries were not kind to Fitzgerald, mentioning how he had wasted his life and talent.

Posthumously, Edmund Wilson edited *The Last Tycoon* and facilitated its publication; he also published a collection of Fitzgerald's essays and letters in *The Crack-Up* (1945). These two publications helped begin to establish Fitzgerald's legacy as one of America's great writers, one who understood the great contradictions of life in America during the 1920s and 1930s.

Zelda died on March 10, 1948, when Highland Hospital caught on fire. It wasn't until 1975 that the Fitzgeralds' bodies were moved to the family cemetery; this time, their tombstones included the last line of *The Great Gatsby*: "So we beat on, boats against the current, borne back ceaselessly into the past."

In 1974 Scottie Fitzgerald Smith, along with Matthew J. Bruccoli and Joan P. Kerr, published *Romantic Egoists: A Pictorial Autobiography from the Albums of Scott and Zelda Fitzgerald*. That same year, Richard

Severo wrote an article for the *New York Times* titled "For Fitzgerald's Works: It's Roaring 70's." In this article, he reports that Fitzgerald's works were earning an incredible amount of money, with Fitzgerald's agent stating that the figure was in the six figures—perhaps seven—annually.[8] Compare that to Fitzgerald's earnings in his lifetime, which averaged between $16,000 and $17,000 annually; during 1932 and 1933, his book royalties totaled a paltry $50.

Also in 1974, the film rights were sold for *The Great Gatsby* for the third time; the Fitzgerald estate was paid $350,000 for those rights. The film starred Robert Redford and Mia Farrow. Fitzgerald's books were expected to sell approximately one million copies in 1974 alone, with *Tender Is the Night*, a novel that brought Fitzgerald scant praise in his lifetime, having sales figures of about 50,000 copies annually. In 1974, approximately 2,400 four-year colleges in the United States were mandating the reading of Fitzgerald's works in their programs, with between 8,000 and 10,000 high schools doing the same. This phenomenon was not restricted to the United States, as the "author's novels and short stories have been translated into almost as many languages as there are."[9]

A granddaughter of the Fitzgeralds, Eleanor Lanahan, wrote books about her famous family, including *Scottie, the Daughter of . . .* and *Zelda: An Illustrated Life*. Near the 100th anniversary of Fitzgerald's birth, Lanahan wrote an article, "Scott and Zelda: Their Style Lives," in the *New York Times*, where she writes that, "Scott's writing still runs as pure as poetry threaded with spirituality, sensuality and sociology. He has influenced many modern writers, but his unique grace cannot be counterfeited."[10]

Notes

1. Linda C. Pelzer, *Student Companion to F. Scott Fitzgerald* (Westport, CT: Greenwood Press, 2000), 1.
2. Ibid., 5.
3. "With College Men," *New York Times*, May 9, 1920, http://www.nytimes.com/books/00/12/24/specials/fitzgerald-paradise.html (accessed May 10, 2009).
4. "Flappers," *New York Times*, September 26, 1920, http://www.nytimes.com/books/00/12/24/specials/fitzgerald-flappers.html?_r=1 (accessed May 10, 2009).
5. Louise Maunsell Field, "Latest Works of Fiction," *New York Times*, March 5, 1922, http://www.nytimes.com/books/00/12/24/specials/fitzgerald-damned.html (accessed May 10, 2009).

6. Hildegarde Hawthorne, "Latest Works of Fiction," *New York Times*, October 29, 1922, http://www.nytimes.com/books/00/12/24/specials/fitzgerald-jazz.html (accessed May 10, 2009).

7. John Chamberlain, "Books of the Times," April 16, 1934, http://www.nytimes.com/books/00/12/24/specials/fitzgerald-dissonances.html (accessed May 10, 2009).

8. Richard Severo, "For Fitzgerald's Works, It's Roaring 70's," *New York Times*, March 3, 1974, http://www.nytimes.com/books/00/12/24/specials/fitzgerald-roaring.html (accessed May 10, 2009).

9. Ibid.

10. Eleanor Lanahan, *Scottie, the Daughter of . . . The Life of Frances Scott Fitzgerald Lanahan Smith* (New York: HarperCollins, 1995); *Zelda: An Illustrated Life: The Private World of Zelda Fitzgerald* (New York: Harry N. Abrams, 1996); "Scott and Zelda: Their Style Lives," *New York Times*, September 1, 1996, http://www.nytimes.com/books/00/12/24/specials/fitzgerald-lanahan.html (accessed May 10, 2009).

CHAPTER FOUR

From Silent to Talkie: The World of Film

History of Silent Film through the 1920s

The 1920s could conceivably be called the Decade of Hollywood. It was in the twenties that talking movies—also known as "talkies"—became competition for and then quickly surpassed silent films. It was in the twenties that movie studios began congregating in one central location: Hollywood, California and the surrounding region. Moreover, it was in the twenties that the number of Americans viewing a film skyrocketed from 35 million a week to an astonishing 80 million—and, with an average of about 800 movies being released each year, viewers had plenty of options from which to choose. By the end of the twenties, 20 studios in Hollywood, with investments of over $2 billion, were creating and promoting films.

Although the overwhelming majority of films made pre-1927 were silent, the notion of combining picture and sound is older than any film. Thomas Edison began experimenting as early as 1877; the December 22, 1877, issue of *Scientific American* reviewed Edison's tin-foil phonograph, saying, "It is already possible by ingenious optical contrivances to throw stereoscopic photographs of people on screens in full view of an audience. Add the talking phonograph to counterfeit their voices, and it would be difficult to carry the illusion of real presence much further."[1]

What *Scientific American* didn't consider in their commentary was the idea of moving film, in which action is captured. This innovation came to fruition with *Exiting the Factory*, a 50-second French film produced in 1895. The oldest surviving film is from October 1888, when Louis Aimé Augustin Le Prince, a Frenchman from the United Kingdom, filmed family members dancing, laughing, and talking in what is known as the "Roundhay Garden Scene."

In Europe at the close of the 19th century, more than one inventor was attempting to merge moving picture and sound, with some of them unsuccessfully attempting partnerships with Edison. In the spring of 1895 Edison released his Kinetophone, wherein a viewer would look inside peepholes to view a moving picture, while two rubber tubes connected to a phonograph played accompanying sound. Edison released a more advanced version of this invention in 1913, one that allowed the film to be projected on a wall for mass viewing. The problems that Edison—and other inventors, both in the United States and Europe—faced were threefold: (1) to successfully synchronize sound and picture; (2) to significantly amplify the sound; and (3) to duplicate the technology so that multiple theaters could simultaneously present the sound-and-sight extravaganza.

In the meantime, theater managers came up with other methods to add sound to the movie-viewing experience. With early films, human narrators stood beside movie screens, explaining the action and putting the images into context. A phonograph might play a recording in the background or a pianist might add background music, improvising as he or she saw fit. As time went by, full orchestras in the theaters sometimes provided accompanying music—often over the voices of theatergoers who were discussing the plot and commenting on the actors. People were hired to provide special sound effects in the theaters and live actors sometimes delivered important lines. Some theaters even encouraged fan sing-alongs to prevent them from annoying others with their chatter during the movies. From nearly their inception, then, silent movies were not enjoyed in silence.

In 1915 the release of *Birth of a Nation* caused the concept of movie sound to further evolve. Rather than having musicians provide

In 1926 the popular "vamp" actress Theda Bara retired, after making seven films in 1919 alone. Bara had shocked middle-class Americans with her raw sexuality. In her movies, the passionate actress often triumphed over the male characters, which was also startling to middle America.

accompanying music that they chose to play, the film came complete to theaters with the musical scores that musicians needed to play as the film was shown. By the time that the 1920s rolled around, "Mighty Wurlitzer" organs were installed in theaters; not only could these organs play music, they could also add sound effects during the films, as well as mimic many sounds that the more expensive orchestras created in the past.

During the 1920s, films became longer and more complex; the variety of genres continued to expand as well, with melodramas, comedies, romances, mysteries, westerns, horror films, biblical epics, and even documentaries. Jobs in the movie industry became more specialized, with writers, costume crews, and so forth each focusing on their specific tasks. Studios signed actors for long-term contracts and had significant control over their careers. In exchange, the studios invested time and money into these actors, teaching them how to act, groom themselves, dress, and more. The studios selected the films that they believed would best showcase the stars that they had developed; the actors themselves had little to no control over these decisions.

Movie Studios

During the 1920s, multiple movie studios were formed, either from scratch or by consolidation of smaller studios. One highly influential

Although studios wanted their stars to look glamorous, it was not inexpensive for them. The popular and fashionable Gruen Guild and Elgin watches, for example, were a pricey investment. In 1927 an 18-jewel Gruen watch with a platinum case and complementary diamond bracelet cost a whopping $1,985.

studio that was newly created during this decade was Warner Bros. Pictures, formed in 1923 by brothers Jack, Harry, Albert, and Sam Warner. They first became known for a film starring the dog Rin Tin Tin and made history when they released *The Jazz Singer*, considered the first true "talkie," in 1927.

In 1926 the Famous Players–Lasky Corporation invested $1 million into their studio; the following year, the company became Paramount Studios. This studio produced films for the "golden couple" of the silent era, Mary Pickford and Douglas Fairbanks Sr. Paramount also released *The Sheik* in 1921, starring Rudolph Valentino, whose smoldering eyes made countless women swoon, and whose untimely death at the age of 31 (of a perforated ulcer and blood poisoning) triggered an outpouring of grief across the country. Paramount also claimed the first-ever Academy Award for Best Picture (1927) for *Wings*, featuring Clara Bow.

In 1924 the MGM studio was created by the merger of Metro Pictures Corporation, Goldwyn Pictures Corporation, and the Louis B. Mayer Pictures Company. A roaring Leo the Lion became the signature opening for MGM pictures in 1928. Irving Thalberg ran MGM until his death in 1936.

Other influential studios during the twenties were RKO (Radio-Keith-Orpheum), which became an RCA subsidiary in 1928, and Fox Film Corporation, which became 20th Century Fox in 1935. Each of these studios also owned its own movie theaters throughout the country. Smaller studios of the era included Universal Pictures; United Artists, founded by Mary Pickford, Douglas Fairbanks Sr., Charlie Chaplin, and D. W. Griffith; and Columbia Pictures. Smaller yet was Disney Studios, which opened in 1923.

In 1920 there were more than 20,000 movie theaters in the United States; in 1927, the Roxy Theater in New York City opened with 6,200 seats, making it the most lavish of the many luxurious theaters owned by film studios. At Grauman's Chinese Theater, stars put their handprints and/or footprints and/or signatures in wet cement, a tradition that continues to this day. The first stars to do so were Mary Pickford and Douglas Fairbanks Sr. on April 30, 1927. Other early stars were Norma Talmadge, Norma Shearer, Harold Lloyd, William S. Hart, Tom Mix and his horse, Tony, Colleen Moore, Gloria Swanson, Constance Talmadge, and Charlie Chaplin.

Charlie Chaplin (seated) signs the contract to establish the first independent film distribution corporation, United Artists, on April 17, 1919. From left to right, standing, are D. W. Griffith, Mary Pickford, Albert H. T. Banzhaf, Dennis F. O'Brien, and Douglas Fairbanks Sr. (AP Photo.)

Comedies

Comedies were very popular in the lighthearted 1920s, with Charlie Chaplin, Buster Keaton, Harold Lloyd, and—until 1921—Roscoe "Fatty" Arbuckle providing the most popular entertainment. Arbuckle served as an actor, a screenwriter, and a director, with his "Fatty and Mabel" films (with the popular Mabel Normand) highly appreciated by movie fans. It was Arbuckle who, after creating his own production company, first hired Buster Keaton; he is also said to have mentored Charlie Chaplin. Arbuckle was accused of forcing sexual relations on a young starlet; her bladder was punctured and she died from peritonitis. At the end of three lurid trials he was finally acquitted but his career never recovered.

Buster Keaton made 14 major silent films, along with multiple short films, frequently also writing for and directing the movies. Keaton was known for his poker face, his acrobatic abilities, and his ability to maintain a sense of composure, no matter how ridiculous the situation. Charlie Chaplin appeared in more than 80 films, both silent and talking; he created unique characters who, although outside of the mainstream, were people with whom his audiences could relate. During the twenties, Chaplin wrote, directed, produced, scored, and edited most of the films in which he appeared. Meanwhile, Harold Lloyd created characters who could have easily been the guy next door, an "everyman" character who experienced what many in the audience had, but in a way that made people laugh. Lloyd was one of the earliest actors to star in romantic comedies and he helped define that subgenre.

Talking Movies

By the time that the 1920s arrived, the most advanced technology for sound in films was Edison's most recent evolution of the Kinetophone. By the decade's midpoint, though, studios were experimenting with other methods to add sound tracks, sound effects, and perhaps dialogue to the silent films that they were releasing at a rapid rate to an enraptured audience.

In 1925 Warner Bros. and Western Electric created a Vitaphone system that was basically a record of the sounds intended to accompany a silent movie; in theory, this disc would become physically integrated with the projector so that pictures and sound merged flawlessly. In reality, this technology was not perfect and was in fact obsolete by 1931. The purpose of the Vitaphone was not to add dialogue to the movie; the intent was to add music and sound effects.

In 1926 Warner Bros. released *Don Juan,* using the Vitaphone. The audience loved the record-breaking number of kisses in the film, which starred John Barrymore, and movie fans enjoyed the performances of the stars but, overall, the reaction to the new technology was disappointing. Nevertheless, Warner invested more than $3 million in their theaters so that sound could be heard, an investment based on their faith in the future success of films with sound.

That same year William Fox of the Fox Film Corporation and General Electric released their own system, known as the Movietone system. In this system, the sound was directly incorporated on the film itself, making picture-sound coordination much more effective. In 1927 Fox released *Sunrise*, complete with its own soundtrack. They also rereleased *What Price Glory?*, this time with a soundtrack and sound effects. Other early uses included a newsreel showing Charles Lindbergh's takeoff in his plane and a five-minute short film titled *They're Coming to Get Me*.

The Jazz Singer

The first full-length talking film was *The Jazz Singer*, starring Al Jolson and produced by Warner Bros. It cost $500,000 to produce this film, which contained significant lengths of silence—but also included six songs and approximately 350 words. Warner had taken a significant risk with this film, financially and reputation-wise; their decision was clearly the correct one, as a $3.5-million profit was made, and Warner Bros. became one of the most powerful film studios of this era and beyond.

Author Paula Marantz Cohen points out how Warner Bros. did not entirely abandon the notion of silent film in this groundbreaking release. According to Cohen, "It begins as a silent film, then moves into speech and song, then moves back into silence, and so on, re-creating again and again its position on the cusp of two worlds."[2] The combination of silence and sound were used in a psychologically effective way; when the Jolson character was still at home, expected to become a Jewish cantor, most of that section of the film is silent. After the character runs away to become a jazz singer on the vaudeville circuit, the film becomes startling rich with sound.

Talking Movies, Post–*Jazz Singer*

The success of *The Jazz Singer* was so significant that the other major studios quickly realized that they also needed cutting-edge sound technology in order to compete with Warner Bros. In 1928 the major studios all therefore agreed to work with Western Electric to create a sound system that would work with all of their set ups—and the era of talking films was ushered in.

Prior to the advent of the talking movie, films were not always the central piece of a night's entertainment at a theater. A short silent film, for example, might serve as the opening act for a night of vaudeville. Once the full-length talkie debuted, though, all of that changed, and the movie itself became the focus of the entertainment. The transition was not seamless, as early talking films were far less graceful than previous movies—because the recording equipment often boxed the actors in, location-wise, on the sets—but the talkies were clearly here to stay.

Studios now needed to hire writers who could create interesting dialogue and actors now needed to sound as good as they looked. Those with heavy accents or squeaky or otherwise distracting voices did not transition well from silent films to talking ones; to quote the *New York Post*, "One of the revelations of the talkies is the fact that the most beautiful nose in the world isn't much of an asset to an actress if she talks through it."[3] Some silent-film actors, whose voices were perhaps fine, could not adjust from using the more dramatic body language required in silent films to the more natural-looking acting with talking films; they did not transition well either.

Hollywood's golden couple, Mary Pickford and Douglas Fairbanks Sr., attempted a handful of talking films before giving up on their acting careers. Pickford's innocent-girl persona no longer seemed credible; nor did Fairbanks's portrayal of pirates, given that his voice was too cultured. Flapper actress Louise Brooks quit working with Paramount, a move that would cost her dearly; she made two movies in Europe, one with sound but, when she returned to the United States, her earlier act of defiance prevented her from successfully making any quality movies. Meanwhile, Lillian Gish moved to the stage, her exaggerated facial expressions no longer effective in film making, and she only occasionally returned to cinema. Neither Richard Barthelmess nor John Gilbert could make the transition either. Actors who did transition successfully included Greta Garbo, Joan Crawford, and Gary Cooper.

Silent films continued to be made after *The Jazz Singer*, but they became less and less common. Charlie Chaplin made two silent films in the 1930s and slowed down his film production overall once sound technology became predominant; however, he continued to make influential films. Other silent film-era comedians, such as Buster Keaton and Harold Lloyd, did not fare as well as Chaplin in making the transition. Charlie Chaplin continued to use the medium of silent film through 1936, when he released *Modern Times*. After that, silent film in the United States was, for all practical purposes, an abandoned art form.

Academy Awards

In 1927 the Academy of Motion Picture Arts and Sciences (AMPAS) was founded; almost immediately, plans were formed to present Academy Awards for stellar movie performances. The first winners were announced in February 1929, with the ceremony taking place three months later in front of a subdued crowd of 270 people, each of whom paid $5 for the privilege—and for dinner. George Stanley created the bronze statuettes handed out to winners. The statues have changed little over the ensuing decades and would look familiar to us today.

The Academy handed out two special awards at the initial ceremony: one to Warner Bros. for producing *The Jazz Singer* and the other to Charlie Chaplin for writing, directing, and starring in *The Circus*. The following year, to add excitement, the winners were not announced until the actual ceremony, although a press release was given to newspapers so they would have the information needed to publish an article the following day.

Silent to Talking Film Transition

The whirlwind transition from silent films to the predominance of talking films took place in just a handful of years, far more quickly than most historical transitions. In October 1930 *Fortune* magazine stated, "The advent of American talking movies is beyond comparison the fastest and most amazing revolution in the whole history of industrial revolutions."[4]

In more recent years, there has been a revived interest in the graceful, ballet-like nature of quality silent films. In 1981 director Francis Ford Coppola added a live orchestral score to the 1927 silent film, *Napoleon*, after the film was restored by Kevin Brownlow. More recently, Turner Classic Movies has restored a number of classic silent films, including four features starring Rudolph Valentino as well as a multitude of other films produced by Warner Bros., MGM, and other studios.

Notes

1. Mark Ulano, "Moving Pictures That Talk: Part 1," FilmSound, http://www.filmsound.org/ulano/talkies.htm (accessed April 26, 2009).
2. Paula Marantz Cohen, *Silent Film and the Triumph of the American Myth* (New York: Oxford University Press, 2001), 167.
3. Ibid., 162 (quoting the *New York Post*).
4. "Talking Motion Pictures," http://xroads.virginia.edu/UG00/3on1/movies/talkies.html (accessed April 26, 2009).

| Prohibition in the
Flapper Era

During the 1920s, increasing numbers of young women began drinking alcoholic beverages. Prior to this era, "proper" women did not imbibe, and certainly not to the degree of some of the flappers. Ironically, flappers began drinking cocktails right when it was—for the first time in the history of the United States—illegal, nationwide, to manufacture, sell, or transport any alcoholic drink. Although, during Prohibition, it was not illegal to buy or to drink alcoholic beverages, this activity was nevertheless indulged in away from the eyes of the law, as these drinkers were clearly consorting with those who were breaking laws by manufacturing and/or selling alcohol.

Although Prohibition was the first nationwide experiment with a ban on alcohol, it was not the first time that some Americans had lived under this type of law. By the time that the Civil War had started in 1861, 13 states had already passed prohibition laws; this number fell to three soon after the war, but then five more states passed these laws after 1880.

Temperance Movement

The notion of temperance as an organized movement in the United States emerged in the 19th century; members of the temperance movement aimed to reduce or eliminate the consumption of alcoholic beverages. Early proponents of temperance tended to be women who spoke out against alcohol after suffering from neglect or abuse from husbands and fathers—or perhaps even sons—who had overindulged in liquor consumption. Proponents of temperance often believed that strong drink led to increases in crime and was immoral, and they believed that an alcohol-free society or at least an alcohol-restrained society would be an idyllic way of life.

Some men also advocated for abstinence from alcohol, including John Bartholomew Gough. After his mother's death in 1835, Gough began drinking heavily, which continued until he joined with the temperance movement in 1842. As a member of the temperance movement, he pleaded with others not to stumble as he had; he published material that expounded upon his beliefs, including these books: *Temperance Addresses* (1870) and *Temperance Lectures* (1879).

Clergy members frequently fought against the use of alcohol, spearheading the creation of temperance groups around the country; it is believed that, by the 1830s, approximately 6,000 groups had formed, with New York (1808) and Massachusetts (1813) leading the early charge. Organizations that gained significant influence later on include the Order of Good Templars (1851), the Woman's Christian Temperance Union (1874), and the Anti-Saloon League (1895). These groups veered from earlier tactics, which had relied upon sharing information about the moral nature of abstinence, and began advocating for governmental regulation of alcohol.

Legislation Passed

By 1917, largely because of the efforts of people in the temperance movement, a legislative ban on alcohol was being considered. By

In 1890, Carry Nation joined the temperance movement. At nearly six feet tall and 175 pounds, she was a formidable foe as she smashed bar fixtures with her hatchet while singing hymns or reciting Bible verses. She sold hatchets to raise funds to pay her fines when she was arrested for her temperance activities.

January 16, 1919, three-quarters of the states had ratified this legislation, which was the 18th Amendment. This triggered the Prohibition
era, effective January 1920.

On October 28, 1919, Congress passed the Volstead Act, which
specified that any drink that was more than 0.5 percent alcohol by
volume was considered alcoholic. Owning items used to manufacture
alcoholic drink was also illegal. Specific fines and jail sentences were
defined in the act as well.

Factors Leading to Prohibition

Although it may be retrospectively hard to understand how the
temperance movement gained enough momentum for alcohol to be
banned, several factors contributed to this occurrence. Proponents of
the Progressive Movement (a group of people advocating multiple
political, economic, moral, and social reforms, including but not limited to Prohibition) believed that eliminating saloons would greatly
reduce corruption and crime. Medical research continued to point out
health benefits of abstaining, while social workers saw a strong con-
nection between the use of alcohol and poverty.

Many people in this era believed in "eugenics" as a way to improve
the human race. Eugenics suggested that people with positive genetic
traits should reproduce and pass those traits along to their children,
while people with negative genetics should not reproduce. Following
this train of thought, people who drank alcohol and also bore children
were counterproductive to the eugenics movement. One Harvard
professor, Reginald Daly, even suggested that the German brutality
that was evident in their vicious fighting during the First World War
came about because German parents had introduced their children to
alcohol at a young age. "If the [German] baby has not been already
prenatally damaged because of beer drunk by his mother," [Daly] was
quoted as saying in *Munsey's*, "he still runs the risk of poisoning from
the alcohol-bearing milk of a drinking mother or wet nurse."[1]

The passage of the 18th Amendment was seen by many as a
struggle between the old, more rural order of the United States and
the emerging urban society—with the old order desperately fighting
for Prohibition as a way to hold on to their more conservative values.

In 1927 journalist Walter Lippman expressed this viewpoint quite eloquently:

> The evil which the old-fashioned preachers ascribe to the Pope, to Babylon, to atheists, and to the devil, is simply the new urban civilization, with its irresistible scientific and economic and mass power. The Pope, the devil, jazz, the bootleggers, are a mythology which expresses symbolically the impact of a vast and dreaded social change. The change is real enough. . . . The defense of the Eighteenth Amendment has, therefore, become much more than a mere question of regulating the liquor traffic. It involves a test of strength between social orders, and when that test is concluded, and if, as seems probable, the Amendment breaks down, the fall will bring down with it the dominion of the older civilization. The Eighteenth Amendment is the rock on which the evangelical church militant is founded, and with it are involved a whole way of life and an ancient tradition. The overcoming of the Eighteenth Amendment would mean the emergence of the cities as the dominant force in America, dominant politically and socially as they are already dominant economically.[2]

During the decades prior to the 18th Amendment, temperance workers had successfully gotten some alcohol education in the schools, so a generation or two of students had grown up hearing about the evils of drink. Meanwhile, this message was also preached in Christian pulpits and repeated by many of the church members, so the notion of abstinence from alcohol was heard from multiple sources and would not have been seen as an unusual idea; many people may have opposed Prohibition, but the notion was not unfamiliar to them at the time of its passage.

Finally, Prohibition was fairly easily accepted in the southern states, in large part because it was perceived by many as a way to keep the black population under control. In 1914 Representative Richmond Pearson Hobson from Alabama shared this viewpoint, saying, "Liquor will actually make a brute out of a negro, causing him to commit unnatural crimes. . . . The effect is the same on the white man, though the white man being further evolved it takes a longer time to reduce him to the same level."[3]

Challenges during Prohibition

The Volstead Act could be confusing to people attempting to follow or enforce its regulations. Initially, this law limited the volume of alcohol in a drink to 0.5 percent. In July 1920 the act was clarified: home brews for home consumption could contain more than 0.5 percent of alcohol, given that the result was "non-intoxicating." These products "may cheer" but "will not inebriate." Homemade cider, according to this clarification, could be sold to any person—given that he or she already had a permit to manufacture vinegar. These modifications, explained Senator Carter Glass, chair of the Committee on Resolutions, were to prevent the "vexatious invasion of the privacy of the home."[4]

Now that Prohibition was in effect nationally, the biggest challenge was to enforce the new laws. The resistance to these laws, not surprisingly, was stronger in cities, where groups settling there were much more tolerant and open-minded. Support for Prohibition was stronger in smaller towns and rural or agricultural areas. In those regions, residents were more likely to adhere to the middle-class Protestant belief in legislating morality.[5]

People who wanted to continue drinking alcohol quickly identified loopholes in the laws. Because drinking alcohol was not illegal, people who could afford to do so bought multiple cases of liquor shortly before Prohibition kicked in. Others, noting that alcohol was still legal for medicinal purposes, persuaded doctors to write them a prescription.

Plus, a good percentage of Americans—including many young women who identified themselves as or were identified by others as flappers—were finding ways to break the law. At no other time in our country's history, it seems, were so many otherwise law-abiding citizens searching for and frequently finding ways to circumvent the law; they hollowed out canes and obtained false books in which to hide

Reverend Herbert Lansdowne Johnson, dean of Detroit's St. Paul's Protestant Episcopal Cathedral, felt that he could not share his pro-Prohibition views. He felt that way because six out of the nine members of the cathedral vestry "kept liquor cellars." Johnson ended up resigning over the dilemma.

their liquor, and they drank their alcohol in tea cups to look proper in case of a raid.

Perhaps one of the reasons that people were so willing to break this law is that enforcement remained a challenge and so lawbreakers were unlikely to get caught, much less prosecuted. Federal agents charged with enforcing this law were spread thinly around the country, while some officials accepted bribes to look the other way as people manufactured and sold alcoholic drink. Meanwhile, although many people successfully averted the law, others weren't so lucky, and the court system was struggling to keep up with prosecuting these people. What complicated matters even further was the wide range of people involved in the manufacturing of alcohol: some people made bathtub gin for friends and family at home, while others ran their liquor production as a business, having little trouble finding paying customers.

Gangsters in the Prohibition Era

The passage of Prohibition had an unanticipated and dangerous consequence, as organized gangsters set up a cottage industry in which

Prohibition officers raid the largest illegal distillery ever uncovered, inspecting thirteen vats with a capacity of 15,000 gallons of liquor apiece. (AP Photo.)

they manufactured, distributed, and sold liquor in large quantities, infiltrating society at multiple levels. It is estimated that there were literally hundreds of thousands of speakeasies during the flapper era.

The most famous Prohibition-era gangster was Al Capone, who controlled the Chicago market and who had significant influence elsewhere in the country, selling tens of millions of dollars worth of illegal alcohol annually. Another was his rival, George "Bugs" Moran. With this rise in gangster activity came gangster rivalries and bloody confrontations; moreover, as gangsters successfully bribed police officers and other officials to look the other way, the legal system became less effective overall.

Stories were told of outrageous true-life speakeasy characters, such as "Texas" Guinan, a bleached-blonde former silent-film western actress. She was said to manage speakeasies for gangsters, cheerfully greeting her customers with "Hello, suckers!" Police raided her clubs and padlocked them so frequently that she began wearing a necklace made of padlocks.

Antiprohibition Movement

As the 1920s progressed, increasing numbers of groups formed to overturn the 18th Amendment. Some believed that alcohol consumption was a state and/or local issue, not a matter for a national constitutional amendment, while others simply believed that Prohibition wasn't working and didn't make sense. It clearly didn't eliminate the consumption of alcohol and it brought negative consequences, such as the proliferation of gangster influence.

A common belief is that alcohol consumption decreased during Prohibition. Whether or not that's true is difficult to determine for certain, as there were no official sales records, and no way to know how much bathtub gin was being made in basements and barns. Moreover, the gangsters managing the speakeasies didn't pay taxes on their sales or provide the government with any information to monitor alcohol consumption.

Some information, though, actually indicates an increase in alcohol use during Prohibition. For example, information provided at the U.S. Senate Judiciary Committee on National Prohibition in 1926 indicates that in 1910 there were 100 alcohol-related deaths per 100,000 of the population in Cook County. An uneven decline is observed until there were about 25 deaths per 100,000 in 1920, which was the start of Prohibition. By 1924, though, about one-third of the way through Prohibition, there were more than 100 deaths per 100,000.[6] A statement made by the Honorable William Cabell Bruce indicates that alcohol-related crimes, as well, were significantly higher during Prohibition than before.[7]

Mark Thornton, assistant professor of economics at Auburn University, listed more negatives of Prohibition in his policy analysis, "Alcohol Prohibition Was a Failure." These include the fact that homemade alcohol was more dangerous to consume than what was previously made, and that many drinkers began ingesting opium, marijuana, patent medicines, and cocaine, among other dangerous substances, during this era. He also concludes that, had Prohibition not been repealed in 1933, alcohol consumption was in danger of passing any pre-Prohibition quantities. Moreover, before Prohibition, about half of alcohol consumption was beer, the beverage with the lowest alcohol content. During Prohibition, consumption consisted largely of distilled spirits, which had significantly higher alcohol content. Perhaps most telling of all, the homicide rate—which kept increasing throughout Prohibition— dropped after its repeal and continued to drop at a rapid pace in subsequent years.[8]

So, the "Noble Experiment" appears to have been a dismal failure. It did not eliminate and most likely did not reduce alcohol consumption; dramatic health-related benefits did not occur because behaviors did not change in the expected manner; and serious crime was not reduced. In fact, gangster activity flourished during this era. Therefore, many people initially in favor of Prohibition were finding it increasingly difficult to continue to defend its existence.

When the stock market crashed in 1929, additional reasons for the repeal of Prohibition came to the forefront. People needed jobs and a legalized alcohol industry would create those jobs; moreover, the alcohol could be taxed, infusing the government with additional funds to provide relief during the Great Depression, create jobs, and fund other projects.

Repeal of Prohibition

On March 22, 1933, President Franklin Delano Roosevelt eased the restrictions imposed by the 18th Amendment by passing the Beer-Wine Revenue Act, which legalized alcoholic beverages with relatively low alcohol content. It is said that, upon signing this legislation, Roosevelt remarked that it was a great day for a beer.

In December 1933, the 21st Amendment repealed Prohibition, returning the authority to ban alcohol to state and local governments via "dry" statues. Since the repeal of the 18th Amendment, the temperance movement has not regained its previous momentum and, to date, no other amendment to the Constitution has been repealed, giving the 18th Amendment a unique place in the history of our country.

As a humorous side note, in a book titled *Prohibition: Its Economic and Industrial Aspects*, author Herman Feldman discussed how challenging bartenders found their situation to be after dispensing alcoholic drinks was no longer a legal profession. Some of them, Feldman explains, learned another trade, while the "less scrupulous" worked in "speak-easies." He then adds that still others found employment working soda fountains, which

> proved a failure. The men who had been ten or fifteen years at fine bars could not adjust themselves to the kind of trade the soda fountains had. The one thing that all complained of most vociferously was having to deal "with fussy women who changed their minds four or five times." The tactfulness that might have been shown in dealing with financiers and sportsmen was not adequate in dealing with flappers.[9]

Notes

1. Andrew Sinclair, *Prohibition: The Era of Excess* (Boston: Little, Brown, 1962), 47.
2. Ibid., 5.
3. Ibid., 29.

4. "Allows Home Brew Over Half Per Cent," *New York Times*, July 25, 1920, http://query.nytimes.com/mem/archive-free/pdf?_r=1&res=9F02E5D91131E433 A25756C2A9619C946195D6CF (accessed April 14, 2009).

5. George Mowry, ed., *The Twenties: Fords, Flappers, and Fanatics* (Englewood Cliffs, NJ: Prentice-Hall, 1963), 89.

6. "Deaths Due to Alcohol, Cook County, 1910–1926," Schaffer Library of Drug Policy, http://www.druglibrary.org/schaffer/History/e1920/chicago-deaths.htm (accessed April 14, 2009).

7. "Did Alcohol Prohibition Increase Crime?" Schaffer Library of Drug Policy, http://www.druglibrary.org/prohibitionresults3.htm (accessed April 14, 2009).

8. Mark Thornton, "Alcohol Prohibition Was a Failure," Cato Institute, July 17, 1991, Policy Analysis no. 157, http://www.cato.org/pub_display.php?pub_id= 1017&full (accessed April 14, 2009).

9. Herman Feldman, *Prohibition: Its Economic and Industrial Aspects* (New York: D. Appleton, 1927), 324.

CHAPTER SIX

Legacy of the Era

When the 1920s ended, so did the era of the flapper, but many of the events and changes that took place during the decade have had ramifications for American culture for decades beyond the twenties. Examining just four of the many cultural, legislative, social, and economic occurrences from the 1920s to see how they have since played out in American history—women in the workforce, Prohibition, the rural to urban population shift, and the stock market crash of 1929—will help to demonstrate the long-lasting effects of the flapper era on our modern-day lives.

Women in the Workforce

Women comprised 23.6 percent of the workforce in 1920, with 8.3 million females aged 15 or older working outside the home, many of whom started working during the war years.[1] Educated women of the era typically worked in the teaching, nursing, and social work fields and, in 1922, nearly every female college graduate planned to get a job. Moreover, writes Alice Kessler-Harris in her study of working women, "To significant numbers of women, marriage and work no longer seemed like mutually exclusive alternatives. The same heady freedom that encouraged young unmarried women from comfortable families to enter the labor force also encouraged them not to give up their careers when they married, or to shun marriage if they had careers."[2]

Pay disparity clearly existed during the twenties; as just one example, males under federal contract for manufacturing jobs started out at 40 cents per hour, with females earning only 25 cents per hour. Although the pay disparity issue still exists today, a step toward its solution took place in 1920, when Congress established the U.S. Department of Labor Women's Bureau to protect the rights and needs of women earning wages. By 1930 27 percent of the workforce was female, with 11 million working women, and over the next decade women were actually entering the workforce at twice the rate as men, but that was largely because it was significantly cheaper to hire a woman.

Married women who worked faced hostility from much of society during the Depression, with naysayers seeing them as taking a paying job away from a man. During this era, both private companies and governmental agencies would often refuse to hire married women; some even fired married women on principle during this era. The situation worsened when, in 1932, the Federal Economy Act prevented more than one family member from working in a governmental job, which meant that many women—including those working in more traditionally female jobs, such as teachers and librarians—lost their jobs.

During the Second World War, the number of working women in the United States increased from 11.9 million to 18.6 million, as men went overseas to fight and women were needed to fill crucial jobs. By the end of the war, 36.1 percent of the civilian workforce was female, with women receiving higher wages than in the past. When the war ended, though, the average female's wage dropped by 26 percent, from $50 per week to $37.

In 1950, about one in three women worked outside the home. In the 1960s, radical social changes were occurring for women, in part because of a push for equality from a segment of the population and in part because of legislative action. In 1963 Betty Friedan published *The Feminine Mystique*, a book that condemned American society for preventing women from fully participating in the workforce. That same year, Congress passed the Equal Pay Act, which requires employers to pay women and men performing the same work equal pay. This act, however, did not mandate that women must have the same access to jobs as men. In 1964, the Civil Rights Act mandated further employment opportunity equality based on gender.

In 1966 Friedan and others formed the National Organization of Women (NOW) to advocate for women's rights. Women from all economic and social strata participated in the demand for equal rights, which included equal pay for equal work and equal job opportunities. Moreover, over the next several years, the government passed laws that required institutions receiving federal funds to avoid all discrimination when hiring, and the Equal Employment Opportunity Commission (EEOC) was formed. Still, women struggled to enter certain male-dominated careers and women were still getting paid less than 60 percent of what a man would be paid for the same jobs.

The sixties and seventies witnessed the most persistent demands for equality and, as decades have since passed, progress for working women has been steady, with 77 percent of women ages 25 to 54 in the workplace in 2000. By 2007, 46 percent of the U.S. labor force was female and by 2016 the projected figure is 47 percent. Perhaps even more important, in 2007, 51 percent of people in high-paying management/professional occupations were female.[3] A September 2009 article at DailyFinance.com stated that 49.83 percent of jobs in the United States were held by women, in large part because 74 percent of the job cuts caused by the troubled economy affected men in construction, manufacturing, and finance industries, while female-dominated fields such as education and health services grew by 12 percent. Between 2006 and 2009 female workers earned 23 percent less than men, in part because female-dominated fields tend to have lower wages.[4]

Prohibition

The 18th Amendment, which took effect near the very beginning of the flapper era, prohibited the manufacturing, distributing, and selling of alcohol beverages. This act was unpopular with many, a significant percentage of whom disregarded the law and made or bought illegally produced alcoholic beverages. Prohibition did not stop the production or consumption of alcohol; in fact, it gave great power, influence, and wealth to gangsters such as Al Capone who supplied speakeasies all over the country with illegally manufactured booze, and who bribed and bullied law enforcement personnel and agencies to further entrench themselves in the liquor business.

Many who first believed that Prohibition was a good governmental policy began changing their minds about its effectiveness. On December 6, 1932, Senator John Blaine of Wisconsin proposed that the U.S. Congress nullify the 18th Amendment (via the 21st Amendment), allowing individual states to determine whether they would stay "dry" or become "wet" again. This legislation was sent to governors in each of the states on February 21, 1933.

Meanwhile, in March 1933, newly elected President Franklin Delano Roosevelt asked Congress to modify the Volstead Act (the piece of legislation that defined illegal alcoholic beverages and listed the penalties associated with manufacturing, distributing, and/or selling

Women protest on October 28, 1932, urging that the 18th Amendment, which led to Prohibition, be repealed. (AP Photo.)

them) to allow for the legal sale of drinks with lower alcohol content. This took place within nine days; on December 5, 1933, the 18th Amendment itself was repealed and people could once again legally buy alcoholic drinks—as long as their state permitted that to happen.

Mississippi, whose government had banned alcoholic beverages in 1907, more than a decade before national Prohibition went into effect, kept a full ban on alcoholic beverages for about three more decades; after that, approximately 50 percent of local governments in Mississippi kept dry laws in effect. Today there are still areas in Mississippi where it is illegal to even drive through a town while having alcohol in your vehicle.

According to David J. Hanson, PhD, from the sociology department of the State University of New York, about 10 percent of the United States is currently dry, affecting about 18 million residents. In addition to Mississippi, other states with large numbers of dry laws include Kentucky, with 55 dry counties and 30 wet counties, with the rest being "moist." In some moist areas, for example, a person can buy a drink in a restaurant or on a golf course; in other moist areas, beer may be legal, but beverages with higher alcohol content are not. Texas, which has 254 counties, is dry in 74 of them, with the rest of them being moist; Alaska has 129 dry towns, of which 32 of them have laws making it illegal to even possess alcoholic beverages.[5]

Locales with modern-day dry laws are often trying to reduce the amount of accidents caused by drunk drivers; now, however, as it was in the 1920s, the benefits of prohibiting alcohol are not always clear. Some studies show that dry towns and counties in fact have more alcohol-related accidents, most likely because people wishing to consume alcohol must drive further from home to obtain the alcohol; if consumed on site, these drinkers have a longer drive home.[6]

Echoes of Prohibition have been heard in more modern times in other ways, too, including debates over the appropriateness of advertising alcoholic beverages and the implementation of legal limitations of that advertising. Another similar debate is over the legalization of marijuana and other drugs that are currently illegal. Marijuana advocates include those who believe that the substance should be legalized for everyone, as well as those who believe that it should be legalized for medicinal purposes, just as alcohol remained legal during Prohibition if a doctor's prescription was obtained.[7]

Rural to Urban Population Shift

In 1920 the United States had—for the first time ever—more people living in urban areas than rural areas. During the 1920s a large number of black Americans left the rural South for city life and its manufacturing jobs; a second migration occurred between 1941 through 1968. The change for black Americans was significant; in 1920 more than 90 percent of them lived in rural towns but, by 1990, more than 90 percent lived in cities.

Immigrants from Asia, the Caribbean, and Latin America, among other places, changed the racial and ethnic demographics of cities in America, as well, especially when the Immigration and Nationality Act of 1965 lifted the national origin quotas that had existed since 1924.

Inner cities became increasingly filled with those living in poverty, as people with the smallest amount of resources moved to them; governments created subsidized housing projects for them, and the poorest residents often had little to no choice but to live in them to avoid becoming homeless. Increased crime was a frequent, unwanted result in the inner cities.

By 1980 a significant percentage of white Americans and other Americans with sufficient financial resources moved away from the core of cities, moving to one of the increasing numbers of suburban areas located around major cities. Suburban living combined some of the best of city life, with stores and safety forces relatively close by, with some of the benefits of rural life, including less congestion and crime. Downtown areas were no longer the centers of business transactions, as shopping centers were built closer to where suburban residents lived.

Neighborhoods became, to a degree, racially segregated; not by law, but by choices made by residents and the affordability of certain neighborhoods. This situation remained, even when some people with sufficient resources from racial minority groups moved to the suburbs and when some whites, also with financial resources, returned to the cities. Because of these types of situations, by the end of the twentieth century, some governments (Portland, Oregon, and Minneapolis, Minnesota, being the most notable) experimented with metropolitan forms of governments intended to rein in "suburban sprawl." These attempts, however, have been the exceptions to the rule.[8]

By 2005 81 percent of Americans lived in urban regions (including suburban areas), with only 19 percent left in rural areas. There are now 51 metropolitan areas in the United States containing at least 1 million people within the urban and suburban regions; New York City proper boasts a population of 8.2 million (with a metropolitan area population of nearly 19 million) and, Los Angeles, 3.9 million (with a metropolitan area population of nearly 13 million).

Stock Market Crash of 1929

The flapper era ended in perhaps the most dramatic way possible, with a decade dedicated to fun and glamour crashing economically, putting a stop to the majority of the pleasurable activities associated with the twenties. The stock market is considered to have "crashed" on Thursday, October 24, 1929, about eight weeks after the Dow Jones Industrial Average reached an all-time high of 381.2 on September 3, 1929.

On that Thursday, now called "Black Thursday," the market ended at 299.5, which was a 21 percent decline from September's high. In a twenty-four-hour period, the market had fallen by 33 points (a 9 percent fall) with trading occurring at a pace three times that of the average for 1929; a financial panic was occurring and people were desperate to sell off stocks that could turn out to be worthless. The values of stocks dropped further on the following Tuesday and Wednesday; by November 13, the market had dropped to 199, leading to a deep economic depression. By 1932 stocks had lost about 90 percent of their precrash value.

No one can say, with certainty, why all of this economic disaster happened. One factor may be that, in the twenties, people were frequently buying stocks on margin, meaning that they would pay $1 for every $10 worth of stock; when stocks rose in value, stockholders appreciably gained wealth but, when stocks lost value, stockholders' wealth basically crashed.

Professor Harold Bierman Jr. of Cornell University provides a more complex explanation, stating that one of the primary causes was the attempt by important people and the media to stop market speculators. A second probable cause was the great expansion of investment trusts, public utility holding companies, and the amount of margin buying, all of which fueled the purchase of public utility stocks, and drove up their prices. Public utilities, utility holding companies, and investment trusts were all highly levered using large amounts of debt and preferred stock. These factors seem to have set the stage for the triggering event. This sector was vulnerable to the arrival of bad news regarding utility regulation. In October 1929, the bad news arrived and utility stocks fell dramatically. After the utilities decreased in price, margin buyers had to sell and there was then panic selling of all stocks.[9]

The country was plunged into what is now called the Great Depression. From 1929 through 1933, unemployment skyrocketed from 3 percent to 25 percent, with 37 percent of all nonfarm workers completely without work. Meanwhile, the nation's output decreased by more than 25 percent and prices fell more than 30 percent. By 1933 the economy had bottomed out; in March 1933, the newly elected President Roosevelt initiated the New Deal, a plan to pull the country out of the economic depression and, in June 1933, Congress passed the National Industrial Recovery Act. Economic recovery was progressing, albeit slowly, when, in May 1937, national output fell 33 percent. Over the next 12-month period, prices fell 11 percent as the second wave of the depression hit. Throughout the thirties, people starved, lost their homes, and otherwise suffered great deprivation.

Because of the depth of the suffering, the federal government became increasingly involved in solving the problems and building in economic safeguards in multiple ways, most notably by creating the Social Security program; passing the Wagner Act, which regulated labor negotiations between employers and employees; and increasing the number of governmental jobs to put Americans back to work. In the 1920s, there were approximately 550,000 paid civilian governmental employees; by 1939, the figure was reaching one million. The following year, there were nearly 105,000,000 civilian governmental employees.

Other elements of the New Deal included banking reforms, emergency relief programs, and aid to tenant farmers and migrant workers. When the United States entered the Second World War in 1941, the depression effectively ended. Although there have been recessions since, some of them significant, the United States has not entered into a full-scale economic depression since the Great Depression. The economic woes of the twenty-first century (2008–2009) have in some ways been compared to the Great Depression, but the economy has remained at a recession level to date. It is to be hoped that the lessons learned during the stock market crash of 1929 and the ensuing depression will help prevent that significant of economic disaster from happening again in America.

Conclusion

The twenties have made an impact on multiple areas of American culture, not limited solely to the four detailed above. Certainly the role of women in the United States has never been the same since the flapper era, an era in which young women participated more fully in American culture than ever before. It was in that era that women obtained an increased amount of buying power, something that has continued to grow. They have also enjoyed some of the illicit pleasures previously denied to "proper" women, such as the consumption of alcohol, smoking of cigarettes, dancing to wild jazz music, and more. Finally, they gained the freedom to display sexiness and sexual behavior to a degree never before witnessed.

To suggest that all women of the era lived the life of a flapper would be incorrect. To suggest that the women who lived the flapper lifestyle enjoyed carefree pleasure every day and night would also be a disservice. To suggest that all flapper behaviors should be emulated by modern-day women is not the intention of this book. To suggest that flappers were thoroughly modern when comparing them to twenty-first-century females in the United States would be an incorrect statement. To suggest that flappers were fighting for equality for themselves, their daughters, and their granddaughters would be a false portrayal of most of these women.

Nevertheless, the women of the 1920s, in numerous ways, were the first modern women, living public lives in American society as they voted, held office, and otherwise worked, dated, played, and traveled, and as they challenged many of the restrictions that had bound their mothers and grandmothers. For that, we owe them a bottom-of-our-heart thanks—and their rightful place in our history books.

Notes

1. It is difficult to compare figures of working women from 1910 to later years; in 1910 women who lived on a farm were considered working women but in later years these women were not counted in the statistics.
2. Alice Kessler-Harris, *Out to Work: A History of Wage-Earning Women in the United States* (Oxford: Oxford University Press, 1983), 227.
3. U.S. Department of Labor, Women's Bureau, http://www.dol.gov/wb/stats/main.htm (accessed April 7, 2009).
4. Bruce Watson, "Rosie the Riveter Redux: Women on Track to Dominate the Job Market," September 3, 2009, http://www.dailyfinance.com/2009/09/03/rosie-the-riveter-redux-women-on-track-to-dominate-the-job-mark (accessed September 4, 2009).
5. David J. Hanson, "Dry Counties," Alcohol Problems and Solutions, http://www2.potsdam.edu/hansondj/Controversies/1140551076.html (accessed May 25, 2009).
6. David J. Hanson, "Dry County Traffic Crashes," Alcohol Problems and Solutions, http://www2.potsdam.edu/hansondj/DrivingIssues/1070545671.html (accessed May 25, 2009).
7. "Women in the Workplace" (Issue), Gale Encyclopedia of U.S. Economic History, The Gale Group Inc., 2000, HighBeam Research, http://www.highbeam.com (accessed May 25, 2009).
8. Paul S. Boyer, "Urbanization," The Oxford Companion to United States History, 2001, http://www.encyclopedia.com/doc/1O119-Urbanization.html (accessed May 25, 2009).
9. Harold Bierman Jr., "The 1929 Stock Market Crash," EH.net, http://eh.net/encyclopedia/article/Bierman.Crash (accessed May 25, 2009).

Biographical Sketches

Robert Benchley

Robert Benchley served as a core member of the Algonquin Round Table, a group of writers and editors who met regularly for lunch at the Algonquin Hotel in New York from 1919 until about 1927. This group is credited with writing numerous bestselling books, popular plays, and more. Well known for his humorous essays, Benchley was also an actor, film critic, radio performer, and movie maker. The books that he published were generally compilations of his humorous columns and stories.

Tracy Chevalier describes Benchley's appeal in this manner: "This comic representation of himself as a bumbling, insecure, somewhat neurotic, middle-class American male challenged to comprehend and cope with the rapid social and technological changes of his time was central to his popular appeal, as both a writer and a performer."[1] Benchley's most famous quote may be "It took me fifteen years to discover I had no talent for writing, but I couldn't give it up because by that time I was too famous."

Born on September 15, 1889, in Worcester, Massachusetts, to Charles and Maria Jane (Moran) Benchley, Robert did not recall a happy childhood, remembering bee stings, feelings of terror during

Author and actor Robert C. Benchley in an undated photo. (AP Photo.)

Fourth of July fireworks, and more. In a spirit of parody and hyper-bole, Benchley often wrote about his childhood and life in greatly exaggerated ways, claiming to have written *Tale of Two Cities*, mar-ried Princess Anastasia of Portugal, and begun *Les Miserables* for Victor Hugo, among other whoppers. In a more true-to-life description, Benchley shared how he left his first day of kindergar-ten after a girl pulled his chair out from underneath him—and then how his mother brought him right back to school. As he continued on in school, this scenario often repeated itself, except that Benchley would be sent home from class for various misdeeds, only to have his mother return him.

In 1898 tragedy struck the Benchley family as Robert's older brother, Edmund, died in action in the Spanish-American War. Benchley looked up to Edmund, so this was a particularly painful loss.

Benchley attended South High School from 1904 through 1907, transferring to Phillips Exeter Academy, thanks to the influence and funding of the woman who had been Edmund's fiancée, Lillian Duryea. At this academy, Benchley joined the drama club, acting in plays, and he created illustrations for its publications. Duryea then helped Benchley to get accepted to Harvard University, where he served as editor of the *Harvard Lampoon*. During his senior year, he wrote a daily column at the *Boston Journal*. On June 6, 1914, Benchley married Gertrude Darling; the couple had two sons, Nathaniel and Robert Jr.

Moving to New York, Benchley began participating in the Algonquin Round Table, and working for *Vanity Fair, Life,* and *New Yorker*; he wrote drama columns for the *New Yorker* through January 1940.

In 1935 his short film, *How to Sleep*, won an Academy Award for Best Short Subject. In November 1938 he and bandleader Artie Shaw began their radio show, *Melody and Madness*, on CBS's *Old Gold Program*, which lasted three years. Benchley also guest-starred on other radio programs, including Bing Crosby's show.

Benchley appeared in 48 short films and had supporting roles in 38 feature-length films, some of which he also wrote. One of them was *The Treasurer's Report* (1928), one of the first all-talking films made; it should be noted that Benchley also helped to write dozens of other screenplays.[2]

Benchley died on November 21, 1945. In 1955 his son Nathaniel published *Robert Benchley: A Biography.*

Notes

1. Tracy Chevalier, *Encyclopedia of the Essay* (London: Fitzroy Dearborn Publishers, 1997), 74.
2. Nathaniel Benchley, "About Robert Benchley," http://www.natbenchley.com/robert_benchley.htm (accessed February 20, 2009).

Clara Bow

Clara Bow was the actress who became known as the "It Girl" after appearing in the movie *It*, created by screenwriter Elinor Glyn. This film was the most popular of its time, breaking attendance records throughout the country. Author F. Scott Fitzgerald called Bow the "quintessential" flapper, "pretty, impudent, superbly assured," as well as "world-wise" and "briefly clad."[1]

An undated file photo of American film actresses Clara Bow, the original "It Girl" (left), and Esther Ralston. (AP Photo.)

Bow—born on July 29, 1905—grew up in a grim household with a schizophrenic mother (Sarah) who once stood over Bow with a knife while she awoke, and an abusive father (Robert) who only sporadically worked. Clara was the only child in the Bow family who survived infancy.

Bow dropped out of school in the eighth grade to help support her family financially. Winning a contest allowed her to act in a film; although her entire part was cut out before it was shown, Bow continued to seek acting roles, first on the East Coast and then in Hollywood. In 1924 alone she appeared in 24 films and in 1925, 14 films. A *Time* magazine article described Bow: "She had enormous saucer eyes, dimpled knees, bee-stung lips and a natural boop-poop-a-doop style. She was the cat's pajamas, the gnat's knees, and the U.S.'s favorite celluloid love goddess."[2]

In 1927 Bow had a supporting role in *Wings*, the first film to win an Academy Award for Best Picture. In it she briefly appears topless as two men break into her room. The following year, she starred in *It* and became one of the country's most sought-after actresses, receiving approximately 45,000 fan letters in a single month. That meant, though, that she was working grueling 90-hour weeks, which eventually caused her to collapse from exhaustion.

When talkies began replacing silent films, Bow's lack of education became apparent. She struggled to memorize lines and her voice was not appealing. That was not, however, the only stress in her life. In 1931 Bow accused her former secretary, Daisy DeVoe, of embezzling $16,000 from her. When DeVoe went to trial, she regaled those in attendance with stories of Bow's love affairs. Bow therefore collapsed again, this time spending time in a sanitarium. During her time away from acting, she married actor Rex Bell.

When Bow returned to Hollywood in 1932 she appeared in *Call Her Savage*, a shocking film for its day, featuring homosexuality, prostitution, and sadism. Two years later, she retired permanently from acting. Bow and her husband had two sons.

Unfortunately for Bow, she continued to suffer psychologically, and it was eventually determined that she was schizophrenic. Through therapy, she recalled being brutally raped by her father. Bow spent the rest of her life struggling with her mental illness. Rex Bell, who became lieutenant governor of Nevada, eventually separated from his wife.

In a letter to gossip columnist Hedda Hopper, Bow passed on the "It" torch not to Elizabeth Taylor or to Brigette Bardot, but "to [Marilyn] Monroe."[3] Bow died of a heart attack on September 27, 1965. It was said that she was watching a Gary Cooper film when she died.

Notes

1. Denise Lowe, *An Encyclopedic Dictionary of Women in Early American Films* (New York: Haworth Press, 2005), 79.
2. "The Girl Who Had IT," *Time*, October 8, 1965, http://www.time.com/time/magazine/article/0,9171,842186,00.html (accessed January 30, 2009).
3. Ibid.

Mary Louise Brooks

Louise Brooks starred in 24 movies from 1925 through 1938, most notably the silent films *Pandora's Box* and *Diary of a Lost Girl*. These movies, directed by the German G. W. (Georg Wilhelm) Pabst, were both released in 1929 and are now considered among the masterpieces of silent film. Brooks was called the "most dazzling and haunting starlet of the twilight period of silent movies," and she personified the flapper on the big screen.[1] While many contemporaries of hers appear to our modern eyes to be overacting, she seems natural on film. As Brooks was a professional dancer, she often appears to be gliding gracefully across the screen.

Brooks is best known for portraying Lulu, a sexually charged character, in *Pandora's Box*; this film most likely contains the first openly lesbian scene in cinema, where actress Alice Roberts in the role of Countess Geschwitz attempts to seduce Lulu.[2]

Brooks was born in Cherryvale, Kansas, on November 14, 1906, to Leonard Porter Brooks, a well-read lawyer who played the violin, and Myra Rude Brooks, a talented pianist and bibliophile who was almost half her husband's age. Louise was the second of four children; she had an older brother Martin (b. 1905), a younger brother, Theodore (b. 1912), and a younger sister, June (b. 1914). Myra Brooks, who had helped raise her five younger siblings, swore that her own children would raise themselves; according to Louise, that's exactly what happened. Brooks claims that, even after she had confessed to smashing part of her mother's best set of Havilland china, her mother simply replied, "Now, dear, don't bother me when I am memorizing Bach."[3]

Encouraged by her mother, Louise began dancing at the age of 10. Myra decided to have her daughter's long black braids cut and shaped into a short bob with bangs. After Brooks was kicked out of her dancing class for being "spoiled, bad-tempered, and insulting," she attended a dancing performance given by Ted Shawn and Ruth St. Denis. At the age of 15, Brooks began taking dance lessons from Shawn and St. Denis in New York, at one of the country's top dancing schools. There Brooks became friends with Martha Graham. She also began performing with the renowned Denishawn troupe.

While in New York, Brooks decided that she wanted to overcome her flat, Midwestern Kansas accent and to learn to speak "clean, unlabeled English." She relied on a soda jerk at a Broadway drugstore to help her. To learn restaurant etiquette, she asked waiters the proper way to eat the various foods that they served, and she sought the advice of salesclerks to learn how to dress appropriately to highlight her petite dancer's body.

In 1924 she became a chorus girl in *George White's Scandals*; that same year, she became the first woman to dance the Charleston in London. In 1925 Brooks performed as a specialty dancer in the Ziegfeld Follies. Her first film was *The Street of Forgotten Men*, where she had a minor part; no print of this 1925 movie is known to exist. After she appeared in that movie, both MGM and Paramount offered her a five-year film contract; she chose to sign with the latter. Throughout her career, though, she would display irresponsible behavior, which caused her to get fired more than once. Probably because of the way she was reared by her parents, she never gained significant self-discipline.

Flappers enthusiastically danced the Charleston. This dance combined kicks, crossing hands over the knees, and bending and straightening up to the beat of the music. The Charleston became so popular that it is remembered as one of the signatures of the 1920s decade.

Brooks had an affair with actor Charlie Chaplin in 1925 and married director Edward Sutherland in 1926, divorcing him two years later. She had a long-term affair with George Preston Marshall, but they never married. Another brief marriage took place in 1933, when she wed millionaire Deering Davis, an excellent dancer; she divorced him five months later.

Brooks's film career ended in 1938. After that, she lived several years in obscurity, a "cloudy, gin-drowned, hand-to-mouth existence with generous helpings of despair."[4] By 1954, though, she began writing and publishing her work in multiple venues. Shortly after that, she began a relationship with film curator James Card.

In 1979 Kenneth Tynan wrote a lengthy piece about Brooks for the *New Yorker* magazine, which revived interest in the silent-film star. In 1982 Brooks collected seven of her published personal essays into an anthology titled *Lulu in Hollywood*. She did not write an autobiography, though, saying that "I . . . am unwilling to write the sexual truth that would make my life worth reading. I cannot unbuckle the Bible Belt. That is why I will never write my memoirs."[5]

Brooks died on November 8, 1985. Barry Paris wrote *Louise Brooks*, an extensive biography, which was published in 1989.

Notes

1. Gary Arnold, "Silent Siren Out of the Box; DVD Celebrates Louise Brooks," *Washington Times*, February 8, 2007, M21.
2. Derek Malcolm, "GW Pabst: Pandora's Box," Guardian.co.uk, July 22, 1999, http://www.guardian.co.uk/film/1999/jul/22/2 (accessed December 28, 2008).
3. Christopher Lehmann, review of *Lulu in Hollywood* by Louise Brooks, *New York Times*, May 21, 1982, http://www.nytimes.com/1982/05/21/books/books-of-the-times-150665.html (accessed July 1, 2009).
4. Bill Blankenship, "Silent Film Star's Troubled Life Began in Kansas," *Capital-Journal*, February 23, 2003, http://www.cjonline.com/stories/022303/art_brooks.shtml (accessed July 1, 2009).
5. Amelia Hastie, *Cupboards of Curiosity: Women, Recollection, and Film History* (Durham, NC: Duke University Press, 2007), 107.

Al Capone

Al Capone may be the most notorious gangster in U.S. history, controlling liquor sales, places of prostitution, and gambling rings in

Chicago throughout the Prohibition era. He demanded protection money while paying off police and politicians to look the other way. Although never proven, seven slayings—now known as the St. Valentine's Day Massacre—solidified Capone's reputation as a ruthless killer who eliminated his rivals without a twinge of conscience. Yet, he had a soft spot for people in need and could be extremely loyal.

He was born on January 17, 1899, in Brooklyn, New York as Alfonso (or Alphonse or Alphonsus) Capone to Gabriele and Teresa Capone, who had immigrated to the United States from Italy in 1894. They brought with them two sons, Vincenzo (who became known as Richard James "Two Gun" Hart) and Raffaele (better known as Ralph "Bottles"), and Teresa was pregnant with their third

Chicago mobster Al Capone attends a football game on January 19, 1931. (AP Photo/File.)

son, Salvatore. Capone also ended up with four younger siblings: Erminio, Umberto, Amedeo, and Mafalda; another sister, Rose, died shortly after birth. Gabriele was a barber who learned to speak broken English; nevertheless, Italian immigrants were not easily accepted into American mainstream culture and the Capones were no exception.

At the age of 14, Capone formed the Navy Street gang to protect Italian women and girls from the Irish who lived nearby. That same year, after receiving a thrashing from the principal, Capone quit school in the sixth grade. As a youth, he also belonged to other gangs, including the Brooklyn Rippers and the Forty Thieves Juniors. In 1917 he began working as a bouncer at the Harvard Inn on Coney Island, where he was part of the Five Points gang and where he received three scars on his face after insulting a woman whose brother avenged her honor in a way that earned Capone the nickname of "Scarface."

On December 4, 1918, his son, Albert Francis "Sonny" Capone was born; at this time, Capone most likely already had syphilis. On December 30, 1918, Capone married Sonny's mother, a woman named Mary Josephine (Mae) Coughlin.

In 1921, after assaulting a rival gang member in New York, Capone moved to Chicago, where he became a lieutenant to the ruthless John Torrio. The Volstead Act had established Prohibition the previous year, opening up endless opportunities for sales of illegal bathtub gin, and the enterprising duo set up speakeasies through the Chicago area. Capone was brutal in his ambitions in Chicago, eliminating people who stood in his way. When Torrio was shot and wounded by rival gang members he left Chicago, and Capone took control of the crime syndicate. Although Capone had no compunction against committing murder, no one was ever willing to testify against him and so he was never formally accused of that crime. The closest he came to indictment was when, in 1926, he was jailed overnight on suspicion of killing three people.

Although people attempted to kill Capone, his spy network was an integral part of Chicago and successfully protected him. Meanwhile, Capone was always careful to have an unbreakable alibi when some of his men killed their rivals. The most notorious murders took place on February 14, 1929, and became known as the St.

Valentine's Day Massacre. Two of Capone's musclemen dressed in police garb when they raided the headquarters of rival George "Bugs" Moran. After Moran's men dropped their weapons, Capone's men shot them more than 150 times. Moran—most likely the real target—was not there and escaped harm; again, Capone had a rock solid alibi. After the massacre, he hired a press agent.

That same year, after the stock market crashed, Capone opened up soup kitchens to help the needy. He seemed to take pride in employing people at his speakeasies and distilleries. Whenever his neighbors asked what he did for a living, he told them that he was a secondhand furniture dealer.

Capone spent some time in prison, starting in May 1929, after he illegally carried a gun. In 1930 he topped the list of Chicago criminals, earning him the nickname of "Public Enemy Number One."

The government, which had to date been unable to imprison Capone for any length of time, began focusing on the fact that Capone had never filed an income tax return and never put any assets in his name. Yet, in 1927, the Bureau of Internal Revenue had estimated that Capone generated $105 million in income that year alone.

During this investigation, Capone's name was found in writing in conjunction with gambling receipts and revenues. In 1931 a federal grand jury indicted Capone on charges of tax evasion. Attempts at bribing the jury failed, and Capone received an 11-year prison term. He served time in the U.S. Penitentiary in Atlanta, as well as Alcatraz.

By the time he was released in 1939, syphilis had taken a serious toll on his mind and body. Immediately after his release, he entered a hospital, then retired to his home near Miami. In 1945 Capone became one of the first civilians treated with penicillin for his syphilis, but it was too late. In 1946 his doctor, who was also a psychiatrist, stated that Capone had the mental capability of a 12-year-old. Capone died on January 25, 1947.

Post-mortem, Capone has gained a degree of folk-hero status. "Capone did things that some people wish they had the guts to do at one time or another. He fearlessly put his life on the line. He was dangerously daring. . . . He fought city hall and got to 'own' it for a while. He gave generously to the needy and lifted the spirits of the downtrodden. He was an equal-opportunity employer before the government made it politically correct and legally binding to do so. He led a glamorous and exciting life."[1]

Note

1. Luciano Iorizzo, *Al Capone: A Biography* (Westport, CT: Greenwood Press, 2003), 104.

Charlie Chaplin

Charles Spencer Chaplin had a long and successful career in films, appearing in more than 80, and becoming one of the most popular silent-film stars in history—then going on to create masterpieces in talking film. Chaplin created a unique brand of poignant comedy, portraying lovable "everyman" characters who were outside the mainstream of society. In an era when overexaggerated acting was expected, Chaplin found a way to use subtlety to portray complex characters and situations. According to PBS, "Chaplin's slapstick acrobatics made him famous, but the subtleties of his acting made him great."[1]

A *Time* magazine article described Chaplin's effect: "An advertisement for a Charlie Chaplin film was a promise of happiness, of that precious, almost shocking moment when art delivers what life cannot, when experience and delight become synonymous, and our investments yield the fabulous, unmerited bonanza we never get past expecting."[2]

Chaplin was born on April 16, 1889, to Charles and Hannah. Because no birth of a Chaplin was recorded in Somerset House for that date and place, it is possible that "Chaplin" was not the actor's birth name. His parents both sang in vaudeville halls; money was always tight, in part because of his father's alcoholism. His mother, who used the stage name of Lily Harley, suffered from mental illness and, by the age of five, Chaplin needed to step in for her on the stage when her voice failed. He later recalled mimicking her cracking voice to the delight of the audience.

When Chaplin was quite young, his father died; he then spent time in workhouses and an orphanage. Chaplin joined "The Eight

Lancashire Lads," a group that clog danced and imitated cats and dogs, among other entertainments. When he was 10, on January 15, 1900, he appeared in *Giddy Ostend* at the London Hippodrome; he then toured for three years, appearing in *Sherlock Holmes*.

Chaplin toured the United States, impressing director Mack Sennett so much that he recruited Chaplin for multiple films for the Keystone Company; Chaplin ended up appearing in 35 Keystone films, starting with *Making a Living* in 1914. By his second film, Chaplin had created the character of the "Little Tramp" that would bring him fame. As the Little Tramp, Chaplin wore baggy pants, a cutaway suit jacket, too large shoes, and a derby hat; he carried a cane and sported an easily recognizable mustache. The Little Tramp also had a unique bow-legged walk.

By 1916 Chaplin was making $10,000 weekly, the highest for an actor—and perhaps for anyone else—at that time. In 1917 he was given a $1-million contract for eight movies. One New York theater was so entranced by Chaplin that only his movies appeared there from 1914 through 1923—stopping only after the building burned down.[3]

In 1919 Chaplin, along with actors Douglas Fairbanks Sr. and Mary Pickford and director D. W. Griffith, created United Artists, so that they could have more control over their creative work. When Chaplin appeared in a film post-1919, he most likely wrote, directed, produced, scored, and edited it in the studio that he cofounded. In The *Great Dictator*, he personally styled Paulette Goddard's hair so that she had the appearance of a scrubwoman. In the 1920s people bought up Chaplin merchandise, ranging from dolls to comic books, and they drank cocktails named after him.

Well-known Chaplin films include *The Kid* (1920), *The Gold Rush* (1924), *The Circus* (1928), *City Lights* (1931), *Modern Times* (1936), *The Great Dictator* (1940), *Monsieur Verdoux* (1947), and *Limelight* (1957). He did not incorporate speech in his films until 1940 and instead relied upon his extraordinary expressiveness and timing to mesmerize the audience.

Chaplin married four times and had numerous liaisons with beautiful women, often much younger than he. In 1918 29-year-old Chaplin married 16-year-old Mildred Harris; the marriage lasted two years. Four years later, he married 16-year-old Lolita McMurray, who performed as Lita Gray; they had two sons, Charles Jr. and

Sydney, but then they divorced in 1927. The lurid gossip about his divorces caused some women's clubs to insist upon bans of his movies. He then married Pauline Levy—who acted as Paulette Goddard—in 1936, when she was 25. They quietly divorced in 1942. His fourth wife was Oona O'Neill, daughter of playwright Eugene O'Neill; she was only 18 at their 1943 wedding. The couple had eight children together.

Chaplin was not well loved by everyone in America. Later films suggested sympathies toward communists, leading some to boycott his movies; in 1943, he was the defendant of an excruciatingly public paternity suit after actress Joan Berry claimed him as the father of her child. Chaplin was indicted for transporting young Berry across state lines, along with other charges, but all were dropped. Although blood tests showed that Chaplin was not the father of her child, a jury nevertheless ordered him to pay child support.

The FBI conducted a lengthy investigation because of his communist sympathies. Although no evidence was found of any treasonous behavior, when Chaplin traveled to England in 1952, he was not permitted to return to the United States. In the 1960s, a festival in New York celebrated his films and in 1972 Chaplin received an Academy Award.

Charlie Chaplin died on Christmas day in 1977 at the age of 88. The following year, his body was dug up and held for ransom. His widow refused to pay the 400,000 pounds demanded, even after the men threatened to harm their youngest children; police caught the extorters and recovered the body and coffin. One man was sentenced to four and a half years of hard labor, while the muscleman was given a suspended 18-month sentence.

Notes

1. "American Masters: Charlie Chaplin," PBS, http://www.pbs.org/wnet/americanmasters/episodes/charlie-chaplin/about-the-actor/77 (accessed February 7, 2009).
2. Ann Douglas, "Charlie Chaplin," *Time*, June 8, 1998, http://www.time.com/time/time100/artists/profile/chaplin.html (accessed February 8, 2009).
3. Alden Whitman, "Chaplin's Little Tramp, an Everyman Trying to Gild Cage of Life, Enthralled World," *New York Times*, December 27, 1977, http://

www.nytimes.com/learning/general/onthisday/bday/0416.html (accessed February 8, 2009).

Joan Crawford

Joan Crawford began her Hollywood career by portraying flapper characters in 1920s films and was one of the very few who successfully crossed over to a lengthy career in talking pictures. Overall, she made approximately 80 films, modifying her image to adapt to changing times. Her image and memory were tainted, though, when one of her four children, Christine, wrote *Mommie Dearest*; in this 1978 book, Crawford is portrayed as a brutal mother.

Crawford was born on March 23, 1905 (or 1906), as Lucille Fay LeSueur, to Thomas and Anna Bell LeSueur in San Antonio, Texas. Not long afterwards, Thomas left the family and Anna moved to Lawton, Oklahoma, where she married Henry Cassin, who owned the local opera house; there, traveling vaudeville troupes performed. While in Lawton, Crawford became increasingly interested in a dancing career. Around 1916 her mother divorced Cassin (either because he was embezzling or was showing too much attention to young Joan, depending upon which biographer to believe). Anna began working in a laundry and Crawford (now known as Billie Cassin) needed to work to pay for boarding school, where life was harsh.

After school ended, Crawford danced for a living, appearing on Broadway in *Innocent Eyes* and *The Passing Show of 1924*. On New Year's Day in 1925 she left for California, after successfully auditioning for the Metro-Goldwyn-Mayer (MGM) studio. She began appearing in movie roles and, in September 1925, after the results of a magazine contest were revealed, she was given the new name of Joan Crawford. The following year, she was named one of the Western Association of Motion Picture Advertisers' (WAMPAS) Baby Stars.

Crawford received her first top billing in 1927 with *The Taxi Driver* and began being paired with top romantic leads of the day. She appeared opposite Lou Chaney in *The Unknown*; from Chaney, she learned much about the craft of acting. In 1928 she appeared in *Our Dancing Daughters* and fan mail flooded in, making Crawford a star. In 1929 she appeared in her first talking film, *Untamed*. Major films from the 1930s included *Possessed* (1931), *Grand Hotel* (1932), *Rain* (1932), and *The Women* (1939).

By the 1940s Crawford had lost much of her appeal and fan base; in a two-year period, she made only two films. Her career was revived, however, when Crawford won an Academy Award for her portrayal of an ambitious waitress in *Mildred Pierce* in 1945. In 1962 she starred in her first horror film, *What Ever Happened to Baby Jane?*, with Bette Davis.

Crawford married four times; the first three were actors—Douglas Fairbanks Jr., Franchot Tone, and Phillip Terry—and the fourth was the board chairman and chief executive officer of the Pepsi-Cola Company, Alfred N. Steele. When Steele died in 1959, just four years after their wedding, Crawford became the company's first female board chairperson. Crawford had also adopted four children: Cathy, Christina, Christopher, and Cynthia.

Crawford died in 1977. The following year, her daughter Christina wrote a tell-all expose, *Mommie Dearest*, in which she describes Crawford as an abusive alcoholic who cared more about her image than her family. This book was made into a movie starring Faye Dunaway. Some people who knew Crawford adamantly defended her, while others verified some of the events described in the book. Some cynics have pointed out that the book was written after Christina discovered that she was not included in the will, while author Christine Ann Lawson in *Understanding the Borderline Mother* uses Crawford's behavior as an example of a "witch" mother. Although the truth will never be known in total, it's fair to say that *Mommie Dearest*—both the book and the movie—has significantly altered Crawford's legacy.

Duke Ellington

Duke Ellington has been called the most prolific composer of the 20th century, composing approximately 3,000 pieces of music in his lifetime, focusing on jazz. Early in his career, he became known as the master of the three-minute song, which fit precisely on a 78-rpm record.

He employed a variety of musical techniques while composing, and his music was enjoyed in multiple venues, including the "ballroom, the comedy stage, the nightclub, the movie house, the theater, the concert hall, and the cathedral."[1] Well-known songs include "Mood Indigo," "Solitude," and "Sophisticated Lady." Complex works of jazz include *Black, Brown and Beige, Liberian Suite, Harlem,* and *Night Creatures.*

Born Edward Kennedy Ellington on April 29, 1899, in Washington, DC, he received early encouragement from his butler father, who longed for his son to become an artist. Ellington began playing the piano at age 7, studied art and music in high school, and turned down a scholarship to Pratt Institute to pursue a career in music, painting signs for extra income in the meantime.

Ellington first performed professionally in 1916, playing jazz on the piano; he formed a band around 1918—the same year that he married Edna Thompson—and his band performed in Harlem clubs, playing some of Ellington's own compositions. In 1923 he formed a new band in New York City, the Washingtonians. He then formed the Duke Ellington Orchestra. Early hits included *East St. Louis Toodle-oo* and *Black and Tan Fantasy.*

The Duke Ellington Orchestra appeared in an Amos 'n' Andy film in 1930, *Check and Double Check.* They were the first group to record jazz compositions that were longer than three minutes. What Ellington did was to continue a song on both sides of a record—and even two sides of two different records, if that's how much space was needed for a song.

Ellington and his band toured Europe for the first of many times in 1933. Ellington's musical group was still playing in dance halls and night clubs in the United States, but this changed in 1943 when they held a concert in Carnegie Hall, which became an annual tradition. In 1951 they played at the Metropolitan Opera House and, in 1957 they appeared on a CBS special, *A Drum Is a Woman.* The following year, the group recorded with Ella Fitzgerald and appeared with her at Carnegie Hall.

Ellington received three Grammys for the musical score he wrote for the 1959 film, *Anatomy of a Murder*, receiving 13 in his lifetime. Other scores written included the theme for the television show *Asphalt Jungle* and the music for the film *Paris Blues.*

In 1966 President Lyndon Johnson awarded Ellington the President's Gold Medal. When Ellington turned 70 in 1969, President Richard Nixon presented him with the Presidential Medal of Freedom and honored him with a banquet in the White House. In 1970 Ellington's band toured Southeast Asia, Japan, Australia, and the Soviet Union. In 1972 they toured the Far East.

A 1972 television special, *Duke Ellington—We Love You Madly* featured Quincy Jones. The following year, Ellington published his memoirs, *Music Is My Mistress*.

Ellington died on May 24, 1974, in New York City. His son, Mercer Ellington, flew to Bermuda the day after the memorial service to honor a musical commitment Ellington had confirmed while dying. Mercer, who wrote a biography of his father, *Duke Ellington in Person* (1978), continued to lead the band until his death in 1996. In 1998 Mercer's son, Paul Mercer Ellington, began leading the orchestra.

Note

1. "Duke Ellington," *PBS—Jazz*, 2000, http://www.pbs.org/jazz/biography/artist_id_ellington_duke.htm (accessed February 14, 2009).

George Gershwin

George Gershwin created some of the most popular music in America during the flapper era and beyond, focusing on songs suitable for Broadway musicals, but also writing orchestra and piano pieces, as well as songs containing influences of jazz, ragtime, and other popular music genres.

Gershwin often collaborated with his older brother, Ira, who wrote lyrics for his melodies; Ira won a Pulitzer Prize for the writing portion of their collaboration, *Of Thee I Sing* (1931), while George Gershwin received a posthumous Pulitzer Prize at the 100th anniversary of his birth. Gershwin was also known for writing music for operas, with *Porgy and Bess* perhaps the most well known today.

George Gershwin was born on September 26, 1898, in Brooklyn, New York to Russian-Jewish immigrants—Morris and Rosa (Bruskin or Brushkin)—who had arrived in America in the 1890s.

Given the name of either "Jacob Gershvin" or "Jacob Gershowitz" at birth, Gershwin was the second of four children. The Gershwins bought a piano, most likely for Ira, but when 11-year-old George performed a song he'd taught himself to play at a neighbor's house, his parents arranged for him to have lessons. It is said that his piano teacher was so impressed by the boy's ability that he didn't charge for the lessons.

Gershwin lived on the Lower East Side of New York in the era when Bessie Smith, Louis Armstrong, and Duke Ellington performed their magical jazz, the styles of which surely influenced his own musical compositions and piano playing. Moreover, according to biographer William G. Hyland, "In New York there was almost every kind of music, from orchestral concerts and piano recitals—often attended by the Gershwin brothers—to raw burlesque, struggling vaudeville, saccharine operettas, and bright and sassy musical comedies."[16] This cornucopia of musical styles also must have influenced Gershwin's compositions, as he often juggled writing popular music for the stage and for recordings with attempts at composing more serious classical scores.

Gershwin continued to study music and at age 15 he began working as a song plugger on Tin Pan Alley. Publishers hired song pluggers to sing and/or play songs, hoping that the melodies or lyrics would capture the attention of the public. In the early 20th century, multiple influential publishers located their offices on 28th Street, between 5th Avenue and Broadway; this locale became known as "Tin Pan Alley." Gershwin earned about $15 weekly from this job and he also recorded piano rolls of music under pseudonyms, earning about $35 per half-dozen rolls.

His first song, published in 1916, was called "When You Want 'Em, You Can't Get 'Em, When You Got 'Em, You Don't Want 'Em." In 1918, he wrote the popular *Swanee*, which brought him significant attention; when sung by Al Jolson, it became a huge hit, selling more than one million copies. That same year, *La, La Lucille* premiered, which was the first show wherein Gershwin composed all of the music.

Other well-known songs include "The Man I Love," "Fascinating Rhythm," "Lady Be Good," "Nice Work if You Can Get It," "Foggy Day," "S'Wonderful," "Our Love Is Here to Stay," "Embraceable You," "I Got Rhythm," *Piano Concerto in F, An*

American in Paris, Rhapsody in Blue, and "Someone to Watch Over Me." The Gershwin brothers collaborated in creating musical comedies and other popular shows as well, such as *George White's Scandals* (1920–1924), *Lady Be Good* (1924), and *Funny Face* (1927).

In 1937 George and Ira partnered with Fred Astaire and Ginger Rogers to create a musical film, *Shall We Dance*. Gershwin had many more projects in the works but became confused during a concert in February 1937. He continued to suffer headaches and temporary blackouts and then fell into a coma. On July 11, 1937, in Hollywood, California, George Gershwin died of a brain tumor at the age of 38, when he was at the peak of his popularity. Years later, Ira Gershwin oversaw the release of several of the brothers' unreleased pieces of music.

Note

1. William G. Hyland, *George Gershwin: A New Biography* (Westport, CT: Praeger, 2003), xiii.

Elinor Glyn

Elinor Glyn was a screenwriter and author who published 22 novels, three short-story collections, and 14 other books. She is most well known for writing the provocative novels *Three Weeks* and *It*, adapting the latter book for the big screen; Clara Bow starred in *It*. Although Glyn denied that the title referred to sex appeal, that term and accompanying definition became part of jazz-age slang.

Glyn was born on October 17, 1864, in Jersey, England, to Douglas and Elinor (Saunders) Sutherland. Her father died when she was just three months old; shortly afterwards, she and her French grandmother, mother, and older sister Lucy moved to Canada where they remained until her impoverished mother remarried in 1871. Returning to Jersey, Glyn discovered that she did not like her stepfather, but she appreciated his extensive library. Reading his books helped fill in the gaps from her spotty education.

Glyn was attractive. At one party, "four men competed to dance with her and, on the way home, in an alcoholic haze, her suitors threw each other into a lake. Arriving home sodden and dripping, they stripped naked and took baths in their host's best champagne, claiming it would ward off chills."[1] A wealthy man named Clayton Glyn heard of this evening and arranged to meet the beautiful Elinor himself.

In 1892 Clayton and Elinor married and had two daughters, Margot and Juliet. The marriage eventually had problems, in part because of Clayton Glyn's drinking; both had affairs.

In 1898 Glyn began writing magazine columns. In 1900 she published her first novel, *The Visits of Elizabeth*, and this book's success allowed Glyn to travel to Italy, France, and Egypt. She continued to write novels, including *Three Weeks* in 1907. This book features a love affair between an older woman and a younger man, and includes a lovemaking scene on a tiger-skin rug. Numerous critics condemned this controversial book, with more than two million readers ignoring the critics and buying the book. *Three Weeks* was translated into multiple languages.

By 1908, Clayton Glyn's spending bankrupted his family. Elinor continued to travel, though, spending time in the United States, including New York, and in Russia. When her husband died in 1915, she moved to Paris and worked as a war correspondent.

In 1920 she published a book, *The Philosophy of Love*, one of the earlier books about how to attract a man. That same year she wrote the screenplay for *The Great Moment*, which starred Gloria Swanson. She also wrote the sequel, *Beyond the Rocks*, for Swanson and Rudolph Valentino.

In 1926 Glyn wrote her defining book, *It*, and then the script for the film. In 1929 she wrote her first script for a "talkie" movie. That year, she also returned to England to avoid a tax issue in the United States. While in England, she directed films, but not too successfully. She wrote her autobiography, *Romantic Adventure*, in 1936.

Glyn died in London, England, on September 23, 1943.

In the 1920s people became fascinated with Egypt after archaeologist Howard Carter found the tomb of the Egyptian pharaoh, Tutankhamen (King Tut). When the man who funded Carter's expedition, Lord Carnarvon, died, rumors flew about the curse of the mummy.

Note

1. "A Secret Sexuality, Tigerskin Rugs and the Birth of the Bonkbuster," *The Daily Mail*, February 13, 1996, 20.

John Held Jr.

John Held Jr. was an artist who found significant commercial success by creating cartoons, caricatures, and illustrations that precisely captured the era of the flappers. Well-known cartoon characters created by Held included Betty Coed and her boyfriend, Joe College. He also created a cartoon strip called *Bird-brained Flappers* based on actress Colleen Moore, among others.

Held was born on January 10, 1889, to John and Annie (Evans) Held; his mother was an actress of some accomplishment, while John Sr. was talented in art. As a child John Sr. had been discovered by a Mormon educator who was traveling in Switzerland. This educator brought him to Salt Lake City, Utah, where he legally adopted him. John Sr. grew up to become an engraver and leader of a band.

John Jr. showed early promise; by age 3, he was already sketching animals. The Held family would share the story of how they once couldn't find their son while in a mountainous area of Utah, but eventually discovered him forming animals out of the dense clay soil. He also sketched illustrations of Salt Lake City Theater where his mother performed. Young John received no art training other than what his father—and Mahonri M. Young, a sculptor and grandson of Brigham Young—gave him. At age 9, he sold his first wood carving for nine dollars.

While still in high school, Held began working as a cartoonist at the *Salt Lake Tribune*, leaving Utah in 1910 to move to New York City with a friend, Harold Ross, who went on to create the *New Yorker* magazine, and Mahonri Young. When the trio arrived in New York, Held had only four dollars in his pocket. He found work at a newspaper, and designed street-car posters, and did work for the advertising department of Wanamaker's store. He and five friends lived in an apartment that they called the "Cockroach Glades."

Held soon began selling his cartoons to the *New Yorker*, along with to *Judge, Puck, Collier's, Redbook, Smart Set, College Humor*, and *Vanity Fair*. Some of his work included illustrations for Robert Benchley's drama columns for *Life*.

He served in the Navy during the First World War and then returned to freelancing his cartoons and illustrations to popular magazines. In them, women bobbed their hair and sported short skirts. Some were dancing wildly, pearl beads swinging in the air, with others lounging with long cigarette holders held elegantly between posed fingers. He also created cartoon strips: *Merely Margie, An Awfully Sweet Girl*, and *Rah, Rah, Rosalie*. At one point, William Randolph Hearst was paying him an astonishing $2,500 per week for his cartoons. Held also designed sets for Broadway shows, wrote children's books, illustrated other authors' books, and created sculptures.

Held bought a 163-acre farm in Westport, Connecticut, where he raised pedigreed dogs and thoroughbred horses, as well as geese. When the stock market crashed in 1929, Held lost much of his money and suffered a nervous collapse. He and his wife, Myrtle, divorced and he never regained his previous popularity. He focused on painting, sculpting, wood cutting, and writing novels and short stories. During the Second World War, he served in the U.S. Army in their signal corps in the United States. He also served as an artist-in-residence for Harvard University and the University of Georgia.

Held died in 1958 of throat cancer. After his death, an American artist and writer named Jonathan Held decided to use the name of John Held Jr., even though he was not related to the original artist. Meanwhile, the works of the genuine John Held Jr. continued to be shown in museums, and a retrospective of his life and career was published in the January 1966 issue of *Playboy*.

Al Jolson

Al Jolson was known as the "World's Greatest Entertainer." He appeared in Oscar Hammerstein's shows on stage and he sold records in the millions; the first talking movie, *The Jazz Singer*,

shared the story of his life and starred Jolson. The first Jewish entertainer of this magnitude in the United States, he is credited with intro-
ducing jazz, blues, and ragtime music to large numbers of white
audiences. His legacy has been tainted, though, because he appeared in
"blackface" during vaudeville acts, darkening his face with burned cork
to sing songs such as "My Mammy" as people shouted for encores.

He was born Asa Yoelson on May 26, 1886, in Lithuania, the
youngest of four children of Rabbi Moses Reuben Yoelson and
Naomi (Cantor) Yoelson.[18] The family immigrated to the United
States when he was a child, with Naomi dying when Jolson was
about 10 years old.

To earn money, Jolson sang and danced on streetcorners, using
the money he earned to buy tickets at the local theater. This lifestyle
conflicted with the plan Jolson's father had for him—that of a reli-
gious life. So Jolson ran away to New York to join his older brother,
Harry. There, in 1899, Jolson appeared in a Jewish play, *Children of
the Ghetto*. Around 1901 he performed with his brother and another
man, touring vaudeville circuits together; it was then that Jolson first
began blackening his face as part of his act. A few years later, he
began performing solo.

Jolson appeared in his first Broadway show, *La Belle Paree*, in
1911; numerous others followed, including *Honeymoon Express*
(1913), *Sinbad* (1918), *Bombo* (1921), and *Big Boy* (1925). By 1920
he was one of the biggest stars on Broadway. While on stage, Jolson
would perform whistling tricks and sing vocal scales, calling himself
"The Blackface with the Grand Opera Voice."

Jolson made brief film appearances before *The Jazz Singer* in
1927, but this movie turned him into a star. Although much of the
movie used subtitles, there were four scenes where the actors talked,
as well as accompanying music and sound effects. Other movies
included *The Singing Fool* (1928), *Say It with Songs* (1929), *Mammy*
(1930), *Big Boy* (1930), *Hallelujah, I'm a Bum* (1933), *Go Into Your
Dance* (1935), and *Swanee River* (1940). In 1932, Jolson started his
own radio program. During his career, he entertained troops overseas during both the Second World War and the Korean War.

Jolson married four times; his most well-known wife was Ruby
Keeler of Ziegfeld Follies and movie fame. Overall, Jolson adopted
three children.

In 1946 *The Jolson Story* was made into a movie, with the sound-track of the film selling millions of copies. A sequel, *Jolson Sings Again*, premiered in 1949.

Suffering a heart attack, Jolson died on October 23, 1950, in San Francisco, California. He willed millions of dollars to charities; posthumously, he was awarded the Congressional Medal of Honor.

Note

1. Other birth dates have been given, some as late as 1888.

Anita Loos

Anita Loos was a successful Hollywood screenwriter by the age of 20 and the novelist who wrote *Gentlemen Prefer Blondes*, a book that was turned into a play, then a 1928 silent picture starring Ruth Taylor, then a 1949 musical starring Carol Channing, and then a 1952 movie starring Marilyn Monroe and Jane Russell. This book, its humorous and frank take on sexuality—and the main character, the "dumb blonde gold digger" Lorelei Lee—brought Loos international fame; during her lifetime, this work was translated into 14 languages. Loos wrote approximately 200 scripts; she also wrote 10 plays, 5 musicals, 4 novels, and 2 autobiographies, and she worked on more than 60 silent movies.

Loos was born on April 26, 1889, in modern-day Mount Shasta, California (previously called Sissons) to Richard Beers and Minnie Ellen Smith Loos.[1] Her father was a newspaper publisher turned theater manager. She began acting in his theater, and then she acted on both the stage (in San Francisco, Los Angeles, and San Diego) and in films. By the age of 13, she was writing fillers for the *New York Morning Telegraph*.

As a teenager, Loos began crafting play synopses and a vaudeville sketch, submitting 105 of them from 1912 through 1915 alone, receiving rejections on only four of them. At times, she was the sole breadwinner for her family. Loos then wrote *The New York Hat*, a script that was produced by groundbreaking film director D. W. Griffith in 1912. This movie starred Mary Pickford and Lionel Barrymore. Griffith was so impressed with Loos that he hired her to write the titles for his 1916 movie, *Intolerance*, a film that some historians believe is the greatest of the silent era.

Loos was well read and intellectual, but she was also quite fashionable. A biographer of hers once said, "As one of the first women who dared to hike her hemlines and bob her hair, Loos came to epitomize the flappers of the 1920s."[2]

In 1915 Loos married Frank Pallma, but she had that marriage annulled. After marrying John Emerson, a writer and director in Hollywood, in 1919, the two began collaborating on writing scripts for and then producing films such as *A Virtuous Vamp* (1919), *The Perfect Woman* (1920), *Dangerous Business* (1920), *Polly of the Follies* (1922), and *Learning to Love* (1925). It is believed, though, that Loos also gave him screen credits that he did not deserve and that she financially supported him and his mistresses, much as she had supported her parents years earlier.

In 1925 *Harper's Bazaar* began serially publishing Loos's novel, *Gentlemen Prefer Blondes*; the following year, it appeared on stage in New York. She followed that book up with *But Gentlemen Marry Brunettes* (1928), which also received positive reviews.

In 1937 her husband announced that they were losing all of their money and would need to "live on Campbell's Soup."[3] After making that strange announcement, one that was not true, he attempted to strangle his wife. Escaping from his grasp, she had him committed to a sanatorium, where he was diagnosed as a schizophrenic. He remained hospitalized for nearly 20 years, dying in the sanatorium.

Loos continued to write scripts for the movies for MGM through the 1930s. In 1946 she turned her attention to writing plays, and in 1951 she dramatized *Gigi* by Colette, which opened the door for Loos to work on other French adaptations. In 1966 she wrote the autobiographical *A Girl Like I*. In 1972 she and Helen Hayes, a close friend, cowrote *Twice Over Lightly: New York Then and Now*. In 1974 she published another autobiographical work, *Kiss Hollywood Good-Bye*.

Loos died on August 18, 1981.

Notes

1. Other dates given for her birth range from 1888 through 1893.
2. Yvonne Shafer, *American Women Playwrights, 1900–1950* (New York: Peter Lang, 1997), 389.

3. John Gross, "Books of The Times; Centenary for Author of an Indubitable Classic," *New York Times*, October 11, 1988, http://query.nytimes.com/gst/full-page.html?res=940DE3D8173DF932A25753C1A96E948260&sec=&spon=& pagewanted=all (accessed December 30, 2008).

Frances Marion

Frances Marion was one of the most sought-after and well-known screenwriters from the mid-1910s through the 1930s, writing scripts for some of the greatest films of the era. Stars that appeared in her movies include Mary Pickford, Douglas Fairbanks Sr., Gary Cooper, Marion Davies, Rudolph Valentino, Jean Harlow, Clark Gable, Wallace Beery, Marie Dressler, the Barrymores, Lillian Gish, John Gilbert, and Greta Garbo, among others. Directors with whom she worked include Maurice Tourneur, Frank Borzage, Victor Seastrom, Marshall Neilan, Allan Dwan, James Cruze, and John Ford. She occasionally directed films as well.

Among Marion's approximately 200 movies are two for which she received Oscars: *The Big House* (1930) and *The Champ* (1931). She was the first female screenwriter to receive an Academy Award for Best Original Screenplay. Moreover, one of her films, *Flapper*, caused the term "flapper" to become part of ordinary vernacular— and, after the film was released, countless women looked up to and admired the star of the movie, Olive Thomas.

Born Frances Marion Owens in San Francisco, California, on November 18, the year of her birth was later reported to be anywhere from 1886 until 1890.[1] Marion worked as an illustrator and then as a reporter in Europe when the First World War began. She did not begin working in Hollywood until 1914, when Lois Weber, one of the first female directors of significance in Hollywood, served as her mentor; Weber taught Marion about film editing, costuming, set design, and more.

Early in her Hollywood career, Marion briefly acted—including with Mary Pickford in 1915 in *A Girl of Yesterday*. She wrote a script for William Randolph Hearst, *Humoresque*, based on a Fannie Hurst novel, and she directed a film for Hearst, *Just Around the Corner*, in 1920.

The movie *Flappers* was also released in 1920; this movie portrayed the lifestyle of a flapper named Genevieve "Ginger" King. After Ginger sneaks off to drink a soda with a boy, her father decides to send her to a strict boarding school, run by Mrs. Paddles (Marcia Harris). There, Ginger becomes involved in a series of adventures, some of them with an older man, Richard Channing (William P. Carleton).

Other films that Marion scripted include *Stella Maris* (1917), *Rebecca of Sunnybrook Farm* (1917), *Anne of Green Gables* (1919), *Pollyanna* (1920), *Stella Dallas* (1925), *The Scarlet Letter* (1926), *The Son of the Sheik* (1926), *The Wind* (1928), and *Dinner at Eight* (1933). In 1933, Marion was chosen as the first vice president of a new organization: the Screen Writers Guild.

Writer Sue Bonner has described Marion's rise to fame this way: "With a keen mind, she set out to promote herself 'without lying down'—more by displaying self-confidence and pluck than by ever succumbing to what predatory studio bosses might expect along the way. Her rugged determination in this regard was intellectual, not sexual."[2]

Marion married four times, with Fred Thomson her third and most well-known spouse; he was a popular cowboy star in the movies up until the time he died unexpectedly. He was also the only one of her spouses who was apparently not intimidated by her fame, a trait that she found attractive. Marion has been quoted as saying, "I spent my life searching for a man to look up to without lying down."[3] Her other three husbands drank heavily and/or had frequent affairs; it has been assumed that she felt less admiration for them than she did for Thomson.

Marion continued to work as a screenwriter until about 1940, during which time she observed the power of females dwindle in Hollywood. "I don't think," Marion once said, "that Hollywood will ever again be as glamorous, or as funny, or as tragic, as it was during the teens, the twenties, and the thirties. But that's what everybody says about the past as he grows older and looks back on the days of his youth, when everything was new and exciting and beautiful. Was it really that way? Frankly, too often, all I can remember are the heartbreak and the hard work."[4]

Marion wrote her autobiography, *Off with Their Heads!* in 1972. She died on May 12, 1973, in Los Angeles, California.

Notes

1. Frances Marion believed that her year of birth was 1888, but she was not certain.
2. Sue Bonner, review of *Without Lying Down: Frances Marion and the Powerful Women of Early Hollywood* by Cari Beauchamp, *Knight-Ridder Newspapers* (1997), http://www.highbeam.com/doc/1G1-19423304.html (accessed December 28, 2008).
3. Lisa Black, review of *Without Lying Down: Frances Marion and the Powerful Women of Early Hollywood* by Cari Beauchamp, *H-Film* (March 1999), http://www.h-net.org/reviews/showrev.php?id=2937 (accessed December 28, 2008).
4. Anthony Slide, *Early Women Directors* (South Brunswick, NJ: A. S. Barnes, 1977), 90–91.

H. L. Mencken

Henry Louis (H. L.) Mencken, who worked as a journalist and became known as the "Sage of Baltimore," has been called the "most influential American literary critic in the 1920s," as well as one of the foremost experts on the English language.[1] As a satirist, he often mocked organized religion, most vehemently when discussing fundamentalist churches; this is why he so enthusiastically covered John Scopes' trial when the teacher was charged with discussing evolution in school. Mencken dubbed it the "Monkey Trial," a nickname that stuck.

Mencken was born on September 12, 1880, in Baltimore, Maryland; his father, August, owned a cigar factory. Privately educated, Mencken graduated from Baltimore Polytechnic Institute at the age of 16. He worked as a reporter at the *Baltimore Morning Herald*, starting in 1899, being promoted first to city editor and then to editor. Starting in 1906, he worked for the *Baltimore Sun*. It was for the *Sun* that he covered the Scopes trial and it was he who persuaded the sought-after attorney, Clarence Darrow, to defend Scopes, seeing this trial as one about the freedom of speech.

Freedom was a cornerstone of Mencken's philosophy. He said, that, "The two main ideas that run through all my writing, whether it be literary criticism or political polemic, are these: I am strongly in favor of liberty and I hate fraud."[2]

Mencken served as a literary critic for the *Smart Set*. In 1924, he and George Jean Nathan founded the *American Mercury*, a publication that Mencken edited until 1933—and the latter publication is what led Mencken into making a public stand against censorship.

In April 1926 Mencken published a true story by Herbert Asbury in the *American Mercury* about a prostitute named Hatrack. She faithfully attended church, where she was shunned. Immediately after church, Hatrack would begin to get customers; she would take the Catholic customers to the Masonic burial ground and the Protestant customers to the Catholic cemetery to get serviced.

The Reverend J. Franklin Chase, who was the secretary of the New England Watch and Ward Society, dedicated himself to ridding the newsstands of what he considered obscene material—and he included the story of Hatrack in that list. Chase had had tremendous success in his quest, but when a Harvard newsstand owner was threatened with a prison sentence for selling a copy of the April issue of *American Mercury*, Mencken decided to get involved.

First he announced that he would sell a copy of the magazine directly to Chase, outside in the Boston Common. The Associated Press published that announcement, so a crowd awaited Mencken; people even climbed up trees to get a good vantage point of the event. When Mencken arrived, he was swarmed by people wanting to buy copies of the *American Mercury*; he sold them as police struggled to maintain order.

When Chase finally arrived and asked to buy a copy with a 50-cent piece, Mencken deliberately bit down on the coin in front of the crowd before handing the reverend an issue. Chase immediately demanded that Mencken be arrested, as he was, but he first tossed the remaining issues in the air, causing a ruckus in the commons. A supportive crowd followed the police vehicle that took Mencken to the police station.

Mencken went to court, where, because of all of Chase's previous successes, he expected to be found guilty. Instead, the judge announced that he would read the issue that evening and then make his ruling the following morning. That next day, the judge found Mencken innocent and he ruled that the *American Mercury* did not break any obscenity laws. As the editor left the courthouse, he was surrounded by applause; when he returned to Harvard, he received a standing ovation.

Besides his newspaper and magazine work, Mencken wrote books, as well, starting with *A Book of Prefaces* in 1917. *The American Language* was published in 1919 and focused on how the English language was used in the United States. This book continued to be updated, with revisions published in 1921, 1923, and 1936, and significant supplements in 1945 and 1948. The six-volume *Prejudices* contained essays and reviews of his, while three more books—*Happy Days, Newspaper Days*, and *Heathen Days*—focused on journalism; his autobiography, *My Life as Author and Editor*, was not published until 1993, per Mencken's request.

Other books included *Ventures into Verse, Bernard Shaw: The Plays, A Book of Burlesques, A Little Book in C Minor, Damn: A Book of Calumny, Heliogablus, Making a President, New Dictionary of Quotations, Christmas Story, Mencken Chrestomathy*, and *Menckeniana: A Schimplexion*. He wrote a play, as well: *The Artist*.

Mencken did not marry until 1930, when he wed Sara Haardt, who died in 1935. Mencken lived for more than 20 years after that. He left his books and papers to the Enoch Pratt Free Library in Baltimore, dying on January 29, 1956, at the age of 75.

Notes

1. "H. L. Mencken: The American Language," C-Span: American Writers II, the 20th Century, 2002, http://www.americanwriters.org/writers/mencken.asp (accessed February 21, 2009).
2. Marion Elizabeth Rodgers, *Mencken: The American Iconoclast* (New York: Oxford University Press, 2005), 2.

Colleen Moore

Colleen Moore was, according to the *New York Times*, "the star of the silent screen who personified the 'flapper' of the 1920's."[1] F. Scott Fitzgerald called her the "Torch of the Flaming Youth." Her films, which number around 100, included *The Perfect Flapper, Naughty but Nice*, and *Little Orphan Annie*.

Born in Michigan on August 19, 1902, as Kathleen Morrison, she attended private schools and studied music at the Detroit Conservatory. When Moore was just 15, her uncle managed to arrange a screen testing for her in front of famed director D. W. Griffith; her uncle had helped get Griffith's *Birth of a Nation* and *Intolerance* past censors and the director was returning the favor. After that screen testing, Moore began appearing as an extra in films; in 1922, she was picked as one of the WAMPAS Baby Stars predicted to find Hollywood success.

By 1923 she had cut off her long curls—at her mother's suggestion—and was then ideal for flapper roles in Hollywood. She appeared in a film, *Flaming Youth*, with a bobbed 'do that was greatly admired by young women around the country—as were her short skirts. She wasn't a classic beauty; in fact, one eye was brown and the other blue. Rather than allowing her quirky appearance to become a deficit, Moore sported cutting-edge fashions, becoming a trendsetter.

Moore especially excelled in roles that emphasized her comedic talents. She also appeared opposite cowboy star Tom Mix in several movies. By 1927 Moore was earning $12,500 a week, while the average American in 1928 was earning $6,078.93 per year.[2]

During the 1920s, Moore spent a whopping $470,000 on a dollhouse that looked like a castle; the dollhouse was equipped with electrical power and running water, and boasted an organ, a radio, and a library complete with leather-bound works of literature. She employed "surgical instrument lighting specialists, Beverly Hills jewelers and Chinese jade craftsmen" for this palace, which eventually measured 8'7" × 8'2" × 7'7".[3]

In 1929 Moore appeared in her first "talkie" film: *Smiling Irish Eyes*. She faced difficulties in changing her acting style to accommodate the new format, yet she appeared in eight more talking films, including *The Power and the Glory* (1933) with Spencer Tracy. The last film she made was *The Scarlet Letter* (1934). After retiring from Hollywood, she traveled, exhibiting dollhouses to raise money for children's charities. Unlike many Hollywood stars, she had invested her money wisely and had a comfortable retirement.

She wrote an autobiography in 1968, *Silent Star*, as well as other books, including *How Women Can Make Money in the Stock Market* (1969) and *Colleen Moore's Doll House* (1971).

Moore married four times, never having children of her own. She first married film producer John McCormick and then Albert

Scott, a stockbroker. With her third husband, stockbroker Homer Hargrave, whom she married in 1937, she raised his two children. Hargrave died in 1967; four years later, Moore hired Paul Maginot to build a home for her. She married him in 1983.

Moore died of cancer on January 25, 1988, at the age of 85.

Notes

1. Glenn Fowler, "Colleen Moore, Star of 'Flapper' Films, Dies at 85," *New York Times*, January 26, 1988, http://query.nytimes.com/gst/fullpage.html?res=940-DE7D61030F935A15752C0A96E948260&sec=&spon=&pagewanted=all (accessed February 2, 2009).
2. "1928 Incomes," *Time*, February 10, 1930, http://www.time.com/time/magazine/article/0,9171,738618,00.html (accessed February 2, 2009).
3. "Colleen Moore's Fairy Castle," *Chicago Museum of Science and Industry*, http://www.msichicago.org/whats-here/exhibits/fairycastle/history-of-the-fairy-castle (accessed February 2, 2009).

Dorothy Parker

Dorothy Parker wrote articles, poems, short stories, and more, during the flapper era and throughout the 1930s, which have been labeled as cynical and sophisticated. In 1919 she was a founding member of the Algonquin Round Table, a group of writers and editors who became well known for their dazzling wit and pithy prose. Other prominent members included Robert Benchley and Harpo Marx, but many believed Parker to be the funniest of the group.

An interview with Parker that appeared in *the Paris Review* (Summer 1956) said that she had a "humor whose particular quality seemed a coupling of brilliant social commentary with a mind of devastating inventiveness."[1]

Dorothy Rothschild Parker was born on August 22, 1893, to J. Henry and Elizabeth Rothschild at the family's summer home in West End, New Jersey. Her father was Jewish (but not related to the wealthy Rothschilds) and her mother was of Scottish heritage. Parker spent an unhappy childhood in New York City. Her mother died when she was quite young; her father remarried, but Parker did not get along with her stepmother or her father. Her stepmother then died, as did her father, the latter in 1913. The year before, her uncle Martin had died when the *Titanic* sank.

Parker—who had a Jewish father and a Protestant mother—was educated in Catholic schools, up until the age of 14 when her formal education ended. By the time she was 21, she was finding success in the publishing world. In 1914 Parker sold a poem to *Vanity Fair*; in 1917, she began reviewing plays for them. By the age of 22 she was also working in the editorial department at *Vogue*.

Parker married stockbroker Edwin P. Parker in 1917. Although her marriage was tumultuous, she continued to succeed in her career. In 1922 Parker published a short story, "Such a Pretty Little Picture," for *Smart Set*, followed up by "Too Bad" for the same publication. In 1925 she began serving on the editorial board of a new publication, the *New Yorker*; she also wrote for the magazine, as well as for *Life, Saturday Evening Post, American Mercury, Cosmopolitan, Harper's Bazaar,* and *Ladies Home Journal.* In 1926 she published her first poetry collection, *Enough Rope,* which became a bestseller. She published two more poetry anthologies, *Sunset Gun* (1928) and *Death and Taxes* (1931), and she also published her fiction in an anthology, *Laments for the Living* (1930).

The 1920s were not entirely happy years for Parker; she attempted suicide at least twice and had at least one abortion. She suffered from both alcoholism and depression. In 1928, she and her husband divorced. It was during the 1920s that Dorothy Parker—among other writers and thinkers of the era—protested the conviction and eventual execution (August 1927) of two socialists who were charged with murder: Nicola (Ferdinando) Sacco and Bartolomeo Vanzetti. Protesters, including Parker, believed that the men were being persecuted more so for their socialist beliefs, radical thoughts, and Italian heritage than for the crime of murder. Parker was jailed for one night after protesting; afterwards she remained sympathetic to the socialist point of view.

In 1933 she met with members of the American Community Party on a cruise; the following year, Parker declared herself as a communist, although it is believed that she never officially joined the party.

She married another man, actor Alan Campbell, in 1934; they wrote for films together, working as screenwriters for the Academy Award–nominated *A Star Is Born* in 1937. They divorced in 1947, in part because of Parker's increasing alcoholism and in part because Campbell had an affair.

In 1949 Parker, now nicknamed the "Queen of the Communists," became blacklisted because of her socialist beliefs. She was investigated four times by committees suspicious of her pro-Communist writings. Parker also founded an Anti-Nazi League in Hollywood. She came to the attention of the California Un-American Activities Committee, and then was summoned to testify before the New York State Joint Legislative Committee on Charitable and Philanthropic Agencies and Committees. Parker spoke in front of the committee but then invoked her Fifth Amendment rights.[2]

Parker remarried Campbell in 1950, but they spent most of the rest of their lives living apart; Campbell died in 1963.

Parker died of a heart attack on June 6, 1967. She left her entire estate to Martin Luther King Jr., who died just a few months later. Her estate was then turned over to the National Association for the Advancement of Colored People (NAACP). Her ashes remained in the file drawer of a New York law office until 1988, when they were turned over to the NAACP; they are now buried in a memorial garden of the NAACP.

Notes

1. Marion Capron, "The Art of Fiction No. 13," *Paris Review* (Summer 1956), http://www.theparisreview.org/viewinterview.php/prmMID/4933 (accessed March 28, 2009).
2. Milly S. Barranger, "Dorothy Parker and the Politics of McCarthyism," *Theatre History Studies* 26 (2006): 7.

John Scopes

John Scopes was at the center of a highly controversial trial that began on July 10, 1925. He was charged with teaching evolution in a Dayton, Tennessee, school, which had recently become a criminal offense in the state. The trial became known as the "Scopes Trial" or the "Monkey Trial."

Born in 1900 to Thomas and Mary Scopes, John Thomas Scopes was taught the importance of literature and philosophy by his parents, who quizzed him about what he read. One anecdote about the Scopes family states that, when Thomas Scopes arrived in Texas (from his native England), he brought with him four books: his Bible, his favorite hymnbook, *The French Revolution* by Thomas Carlyle, and *Origin of Species* by Charles Darwin. How ironic if this anecdote is true!

When Scopes was 11, they moved to Danville, Illinois, and then to Salem, Illinois, where Scopes completed high school. He attended and graduated from the University of Kentucky. Scopes then applied for a teaching job in Dayton, Tennessee; he was hired, although some on the school board were concerned because he smoked and danced. Later on, he admitted to attending the Presbyterian Church in hopes of finding a woman to date.

When Scopes had completed teaching his first year of school and summer arrived, he intended to return home to Kentucky until fall. After a beautiful blonde woman caught his attention, though, he stayed in Tennessee for another week, hoping to get a date with her.

During that time, the newly formed American Civil Liberties Union (ACLU) published a newspaper ad asking a teacher to volunteer as a test case in the court system, challenging the law that prohibited the teaching of evolution.

Scopes later recalled that he was playing tennis when town businessmen invited him to an important meeting at Robinson's Drugstore. At the meeting, he was asked if he was willing to be indicted for teaching evolution so the law could be challenged in court. It is interesting to note that Scopes did not specifically recall teaching Darwin's theory in class. He did recall, though, discussing evolution in a general way in the classroom. He also remembered assigning a chapter in *Civic Biology* by George W. Hunter, which contained information about the theory of evolution when he was substituting for the regular biology teacher. Scopes was ill the next day, though, and no actual discussion occurred about this chapter.

On these flimsy offenses, Scopes agreed to be indicted; he believed in evolution and was willing to help fight the law. Scopes would have the services of Clarence Darrow, the son of an atheist and arguably the best defense attorney in America, who earned as much as $250,000 per case. Prosecuting the case would be William

Jennings Bryan, a well-known politician who did not believe in evolution.

This trial was the first to be broadcast live on a radio station in the United States. Reporters traveled from around the country to attend the trial as well. In recalling the media circus, Scopes later wrote, "The town was filled with men and women who considered the case a duel to the death."[1] Surely one of the most unusual parts of this entire story was when a journalist left town and Scopes himself filled in for the reporter at his own trial.

At the end of the trial, the judge convicted Scopes and fined him $100. Using the Consumer Price Index to make a comparison, this would be equivalent to a $1,228.20 fine in 2008.[2] Scopes spoke for the first time after being found guilty, saying that he felt convicted of violating an unjust law, adding that he would continue to oppose that law.

After the trial ended, Scopes quit his teaching career. He attended the University of Chicago on a scholarship and, after earning a master's degree in geology, he accepted work in Venezuela as a petroleum engineer.

He returned to America in 1960 when *Inherit the Wind*, a movie based on his trial, aired. In 1967 Scopes wrote his autobiography, *Center of the Storm*. He died three years later.

Notes

1. "People and Events: John Scopes (1900–1970)," PBS, http://www.pbs.org/wgbh/amex/monkeytrial/peopleevents/p_scopes.html (accessed February 4, 2009).
2. "Six Ways to Compute the Relative Value of a U.S. Dollar Amount, 1774 to Present," Measuring Worth, http://www.measuringworth.com/calculators/uscompare/result.php#, (accessed February 4, 2009).

Bessie Smith

Bessie Smith was an extraordinary blues singer, making approximately 160 recordings of her powerful voice, including collaborations with jazz great Louie Armstrong. Because of her expressive voice, she became known as the "Empress of the Blues."

A 1924 photo of blues singer Bessie Smith. (AP Photo.)

Born on April 15, 1894, in Chattanooga, Tennessee, Smith was one of 10 children. After being orphaned at age 8, Smith and some of her siblings sang on streetcorners for coins to relieve some of their poverty. It is believed that, when Smith was 8 or 9, she performed at the Ivory Theater in Chattanooga. Her oldest brother, Clarence, joined and traveled with the Moses Stokes touring minstrel show; in 1912, he arranged for Smith to also join the tour.

Smith began singing with Gertrude "Ma" Rainey, a woman who was called the "Mother of the Blues." Rainey served as a mentor for Smith, providing her with guidance and training; Smith's earlier performances had more of a folk flavor, which some have attributed to Rainey's influence. Both women were openly bisexual, unusual for the era.

Smith performed in small towns and cities in the south, including Birmingham, Memphis, Atlanta, and Savannah, usually in tent shows because the theaters in the South were rarely open to black performers or audiences.

In 1923 she recorded *Gulf Coast Blues* and *Down Hearted Blues*, accompanied by Clarence Williams; Williams had introduced Smith to Frank Walker of Columbia Records and the latter song sold more than two million copies. During her career, Smith would also be accompanied by Fletcher Henderson, Benny Goodman, Buster Bailey, Eddie Lang, Coleman Hawkins, Don Redman, James P. Johnson, Charlie Green, Joe Smith, and Tommy Ladnier, each of whom was well respected for his musical abilities.

In 1925 she broke new ground for singers, recording a song using a microphone; that song was "Cake Walking Babies." In 1926 Carl Van Vechten wrote an eye-opening article about Smith for *Vanity Fair*; many white readers had not previously known about the blues and its poignant emphasis on life's struggles. During the 1920s Smith was receiving as much as $2,000 per week for her live performances. That said, she only made $28,575, all told, for her 160 recordings.

In 1929 she appeared in a film, *St. Louis Blues*, based on a song of the same name. This movie was banned because of its realism but has been preserved by the Museum of Modern Art in New York City.

Smith had married a Philadelphia police officer named Jack Gee; their marriage was volatile, tending "toward extremes of love and hate" with a "considerable amount of physical violence between the two of them."[1] Gee's name appears as composer on many of Smith's songs, but it is believed that Smith would do this to appease her husband, who had no known musical ability.

She continued to perform in the 1930s, but the Depression prevented many of her fans from attending her shows. Plus, her increasing signs of alcoholism made some theater owners reluctant to contract with her. In 1931 Columbia Records dropped Smith as a recording artist altogether.

On September 26, 1937, Smith performed in Memphis. After leaving the show, she and her manager were involved in a car accident that nearly severed her right arm; she died the following morning in the hospital. Rumors suggested that, had Smith been white, she would have received better and faster medical care. One story said that the doctor on the scene treated a white couple with minor injuries, ignoring Smith as she was bleeding to death. Another rumor claimed that the ambulance driver needed to find a hospital that accepted black patients, but couldn't find one in time. In 1960 playwright Edward Albee wrote about this scenario in *The Death of Bessie Smith*.

Also in the 1960s, singer Janis Joplin, who was strongly influenced by Smith, helped finance a marker for the Empress of the Blue's grave. In 1973 Chris Albertson published *Bessie: Biography of Bessie Smith*.

Note

1. Dick Weissman, *Blues: The Basics* (New York: Routledge, 2004), 34.

Olive Thomas

A stunningly attractive woman who died a mysterious death, Thomas is best known for starring in the 1920 movie *The Flapper*. In this movie, she is sent away to a strict boarding school after sneaking off to drink a soda with a boy; at the school, she participates in numerous adventures, including flirtations with a much older man, and she unwittingly becomes involved in a theft from the school's safe.

Born Oliveretta Elaine Duffy in Charleroi, Pennsylvania, she is believed to have been born on October 20, 1894. Married to Bernard Krug Thomas in her early teens, she was divorced two years later. She moved to New York, where she found work in a department store; there she entered—and won—a contest for the most beautiful girl in New York.

After winning that contest, she began modeling and then began appearing on Broadway in *Ziegfeld's Follies*. By 1916 she had a film contract and appeared in episode 10 of *Beatrix Fairfax*.

That same year, Thomas had a whirlwind romance with Jack Pickford, brother of movie star Mary Pickford. Thomas was quoted as saying this about Jack: "We got along so well on the dance floor that we decided that we would be able to get along together for the rest of our lives." It's hard to determine if Thomas actually felt that way or if the studio came up with that statement to make the relationship seem even more romantic.

Pickford was a child actor and was appearing in films by the age of 13. Handsome and charming, he earned a reputation as a womanizer and, during a short stint in the U.S. Navy he was accused of accepting bribes and was discharged.

Thomas appeared in six films in 1917, three in 1918, eight in 1919, and five more in 1920, becoming increasingly popular with filmgoers. Rumors swirled about the couple's drug and alcohol use and their troubled marriage. In August 1920 the couple traveled to France for a second honeymoon.

In September, while still in France, Pickford called the hotel doctor for Thomas, who was in extreme pain. Days later, the young star was dead. Numerous theories existed about the cause of death, which the doctor ruled accidental. One persistent rumor stated that Thomas accidentally drank the topical mercury bi-chloride the couple kept on hand to combat venereal disease. Some people insisted that Pickford murdered his wife, while others suspected that Thomas committed suicide.

In 2004, an article titled "Mark a Forgotten Grave" was published in *American Theatre*, listing the 10 most neglected graves of American entertainers. One of the two worst belonged to silent-film actress Olive Thomas, who had no family to maintain her grave. A nonprofit group called the Friends of the Woodlawn Cemetery is raising funds for restoration efforts.[1]

Note

1. "Friends of the Woodlawn Cemetery Seek to Preserve Neglected Gravesites of Deceased American Entertainers," *American Theatre*, January 1, 2004, http://www.highbeam.com/doc/1G1-112023735.html (accessed January 6, 2009).

Glossary

The 1920s were the first decade in American history with a well-defined youth culture, wherein young men and women expressed a value system that was distinctly different from the values held by middle-aged and older adults; it isn't surprising then, that, in this decade, youth created a significant body of slang terms to reflect those values—and they used them liberally. Numerous slang terms of the 1920s referred to attractive women, physical intimacies, money, and illegal booze, suggesting that these were of prime importance to young adults during the flapper era. Some of the quite colorful slang terms of this era left the vernacular as quickly as they arrived, while others remain part of our vocabulary, even today.

All wet: An idea that had no merit; also used in a derogatory sense about a person; "He's all wet."

Ankle: To walk somewhere.

Applesauce: An expletive that could be used in mixed company. "Oh . . . applesauce!" This term could be used interchangeably with "horsefeathers."

Baby: Term of endearment.

Baby grand: An especially large man.

Baby vamp: An especially attractive female.

Ball and chain: A demanding wife.

Banana oil: Term meaning "oh, nonsense!"

Bank's closed: Someone turns down a request for a kiss or some other intimacy; the answer might be, "No. The bank's closed."

Bathtub gin: Illegal liquor, which was widely manufactured during Prohibition; could be used interchangeably with "bootleg" or "hooch."

Beat it: A term used to tell someone to go away; similar to "dry up" or "go chase yourself" or "scram."

Beat your gums: Chatting or conversing about something that has no depth.

Beaut: An especially attractive woman.

Bee's knees: Something amazing, whether it was a person, a movie, an object, or something else; used as "Clara Bow was just the bee's knees in *The Plastic Age*, wasn't she?" Other terms used in this sense are "cat's meow," "cat's pajamas," and "berries."

Beeswax: Used interchangeably with "business," as in "What Sam and I did at the club is none of your beeswax."

Berries: Something marvelous; could be used interchangeably with "bee's knees" or "cat's meow" or "cat's pajamas."

Big Cheese: Denotes someone of importance, often a boss or supervisor.

Big Stem: Broadway in New York.

Bird: A derogatory term that could be used for a man or woman, usually in conjunction with "odd." A comment might be "That Susie is one odd bird, isn't she?"

Biscuit: A girl who is generally open to necking and petting.

Blow: A wild party; also used to indicate leaving somewhere.

Bluenose: An exceptionally prudish person, one generally disapproving of cultural trends. *See also* Mrs. Grundy.

Bootleg: Illegal liquor, which was widely manufactured during Prohibition; could be used interchangeably with "bathtub gin" or "hooch."

Bubs: Breasts.

Bug-eyed Betty: An unattractive female; similar to a "chunk of lead."

Bull: Someone in law enforcement; also used to mean "nonsense" or to refer to idle chat; when men talked about sexual interactions, it could be termed a "bull session."

Bump off: To kill.

Bunny: Someone who is confused.

Butt me: A request for a cigarette.

Button shining: Especially close dancing or other contact with a person of the opposite sex.

Cake-eater: A man who loves the ladies.

Carry a torch: Have a crush on another person.

Cash or check: "Cash" referred to a kiss, with "cash or carry" raising this question: Do we kiss now or later?

Cast a kitten: To throw a tantrum; "Take me to the party or else I'll cast a kitten!"

Cat's meow: Something marvelous; this term could be used interchangeably with "bee's knees," "cat's pajamas," or "berries."

Cat's pajamas: Refers to something wonderful; this term could be used interchangeably with "bee's knees," "cat's meow," or "berries."

Chunk of lead: An unattractive female; similar to a "bug-eyed Betty."

Ciggy: A cigarette; used interchangeably with "fag." A pack of ciggies was known as a "hope chest."

Clam: A dollar.

Coffin varnish: Strong, possibly dangerously so, illegal liquor.

Copacetic: A terrific situation.

Daddy: A boyfriend, especially if older and/or rich.

Dame: A term for a female; this term was not in style during the early part of the era.

Dapper: The dad of a flapper; also means fashionably dressed.

Dead soldier: An empty beer bottle.

Dewdropper: Someone without a job who lies around all day.

Dick: A private investigator.

Dogs: Feet, as in "My dogs are tired."

Dog's bollucks: The absolute best of something; used interchangeably with "dog's danglies" or "mutt's nuts."

Dog's danglies: The absolute best of something; used interchangeably with "dog's bollucks" or "mutt's nuts."

Doll: A beautiful woman.

Dolled up: All dressed up/made up with makeup.

Dope: Illegal drugs, most likely cocaine or opium.

Dough: Money.

Drag: A dull date; could be used interchangeably with "pickle," "pill," or "flat tire."

Drugstore cowboy: A man who hangs out on streetcorners in hopes of finding the company of a female.

Dry up: A request for someone to stop talking and/or to go away; similar to "beat it" or "go chase yourself" or "scram."

Edge: A person has imbibed enough alcohol to feel a "buzz."

Embalmed: Drunk.

Ethel: A feminine-looking or -acting male.

Face stretcher: An older woman doing her best to appear younger than she is.

Fag: A cigarette; used interchangeably with "ciggy." A pack of ciggies was known as a "hope chest."

Fire extinguisher: A chaperone who prevented anything hot and heavy from occurring.

Flapperanto: The lingo of a flapper.

Flat tire: A dull date; could be used interchangeably with "drag," "pickle," or "pill."

Flivver: A Model T car.

Floorflusher: A relentless dancer.

Flour lover: A woman who used too much face powder, causing her face to have a pale, dry appearance.

Fly boy: Someone who could pilot a plane.

Frame: To set someone up through false evidence.

Gams: A woman's legs, especially attractive legs.

Gay: Energetic and lively.

Get a wiggle on: Start moving faster.

Get hot!: Encouragement shouted out to a dancer.

Giggle water: An alcoholic drink.

Gin mill: An establishment where hard liquor was sold; another term for a place with illicit liquor was a "juice joint" or "speakeasy."

Glad rags: Dressed up to go out to a club or similar venue.

Go chase yourself: Go away; similar in meaning to "beat it" or "dry up" or "scram."

Goofy: Infatuated with someone.

Grummy: Depressed.

Handcuff: Engagement ring.

Heeler: A terrible dancer.

Hip to the jive: Person who follows cutting-edge trends.

Hooch: Illegal liquor, which was widely manufactured during Prohibition; could be used interchangeably with "bathtub gin" or "bootleg."

Hope chest: Pack of cigarettes, which were known as "ciggies" or "fags."

Horsefeathers: An expletive that could be used in mixed company; could be used interchangeably with "applesauce."

Icy mitt: Rejecting another person.

I'm going to see someone about a dog: A person was going to leave, most likely to buy whiskey.

Insured: Engaged.

Iron my shoelaces: "I'm going to the restroom."

It: Sexual attractiveness.

Jack: Money.

Jake: Everything is fine, as in "It's all jake."

Jalopy: An older car.

Jane: A term for a female.

Jazz babies: Another term for flappers.

Jazzbo: An attractive young man; used interchangeably with "jellbean."

Jellbean: An attractive young man; used interchangeably with "jazzbo."

Jewelers: Flappers in college who try to collect quantities of fraternity pins from good-looking men.

Joe Zilch: A below average student.

Juice joint: A place where hard liquor was sold; other terms would be "gin mill" or "speakeasy."

Kale: Money.

Know my onions: "I know what I'm talking about."

Let George do it: A way to try to get out of work.

Lettuce: Paper money.

Lollygagger: An idle person and/or someone who enjoys necking or petting.

Lounge lizard: A man who spends times in clubs in hopes of finding a female sexual partner.

Manacle: Wedding ring.

Mazuma: Money.

Middle aisle: Get married.

Mind your potatoes: Mind your own business.

Moll: A woman who was dating or associated with a gangster; these women were also known as "gun molls."

Monogs: A male or female who has only one partner of the opposite sex.

Moonshine: Homemade whiskey.

Mrs. Grundy: An extremely prudish woman; could be used interchangeably with "bluenose."

Mugging match: A petting or necking session; also called a "necking party."

Mutt's nuts: The absolute best of something; used interchangeably with "dog's bollucks" or "dog's danglies."

Neck: Kissing and enjoying intimacies with another person; could be used interchangeably with "pet" or "spoon."

Necking party: A petting or necking session; also called a "mugging match."

Nifty: A term for something outstanding.

Noodle juice: Tea.

Nookie: Sex.

Now you're on the trolley: "Now you understand what I mean!"

Oliver Twist: A talented dancer.

On a toot: Binge drinking.

Orchid: An expensive item.

Ossified: Drunk.

Owl: A flapper who is only seen at night, at parties and other social occasions.

Panther sweat: Whiskey.

Pet: Kissing and enjoying intimacies with another person; could be used interchangeably with "neck" or "spoon."

Petting pantry: A movie theater where people enjoy intimacies in the dark.

Pickle: A dull date; could be used interchangeably with "drag," "pill," or "flat tire."

Piffle: Ramble on about unimportant topics.

Pill: A dull date; could be used interchangeably with "drag," "pickle," or "flat tire."

Pipe down: Stop talking.

Pocket twister: A flapper who gets a man to spend all of his money on her.

Posi-lootly: Yes.

Prom-trotter: A student who doesn't miss school events.

Punch the bag: To chat casually.

Puttin' on the Ritz: Dressing or acting high style.

Quiff: A cheap prostitute/street walker.

Rain pitchforks: A hard rain.

Razz: To mock someone.

Rhatz: A term used to express disappointment.

Round-heeled: A woman who is willing to have sexual intercourse.

Run-out powder: Leaving a place without paying rent; can also mean an escape from another unwanted situation.

Sap: A fool.

Scram: Go away; similar to "beat it" or "dry up" or "go chase yourself."

Sheba: An attractive female.

Sheik: An attractive male.

Shiv: A knife.

Skirt: A pretty female.

Smudger: Someone who gets very close to the other person while dancing.

Sob sister: A female reporter who becomes emotional or sentimental about her story.

Sockdollager: An action with significant impact.

So's your old man: An insulting/derogatory phrase.

Speakeasy: An establishment where hard liquor was sold; another term for a place with illicit liquor was a "gin mill" or a "juice joint."

Spifflicated: Drunk.

Spoon: Kissing and enjoying intimacies with another person; could be used interchangeably with "neck" or "pet."

Squirrels: The police.

Stilts: Legs.

Struggle buggy: The back seat of a car, where intimacies could take place.

Sugar daddy: A man who offers a younger woman gifts in exchange for sex.

Tell it to Sweeney: An expression of disbelief; means "tell it to someone else who might believe you."

Tomato: A female, especially a well-endowed one.

Twenty-three skidoo: Let's go!

Upchuck: To throw up after drinking too much.

Voot: Money.

Waterproof: A woman who doesn't need makeup to look attractive.

Wet blanket: Someone who ruins all the fun.

Whoopee: To enjoy a great time.

Zozzled: Drunk.

Primary Documents

1. To the Flapper's Defense

"To the Flapper's Defense" appeared in the Daily Democrat-Tribune *on January 10, 1922; in this article, the British novelist W. L. George shares a positive view of the flapper lifestyle. Although George died at the young age of 43 on January 30, 1926, he published 28 books, with four more books published posthumously. In his writing, he focused significantly on the treatment of women; he was known as a socially progressive writer because of his interest in the "sexual and social politics of much of the late-Victorian and Edwardian period."[1]*

Note that George used this article to good advantage, in it promoting his new book, Ursula Trent. *Perhaps George felt a special need to promote this book as it had, just three months earlier, received a scathing review in the* New York Times. *In the review, written by Louise Maunsell Field— author of* Katherine Trevalyan *(1908),* A Woman of Feeling *(1916) and, later on,* Love and Life *(1923)—Ursula is sharply criticized.*

According to Field, Ursula "learned the ways of a society composed of kept women and their keepers, a society of people who came from the gutter and went back to the gutter. She got drunk; she came to actual blows and a hair-pulling contest with the woman who was the temporary mistress of

the man with whom she herself was living." When she discovered that her
mother was suffering from heart disease, "Ursula is much too modern to
have even a vestige of what those almost incredibly stupid people, the Vic-
torians, called family affection. . . . Why should it? To love one's mother
isn't modern; it isn't 'life'; it is stupid, banal, old fashioned—according to
the self-styled modernists who . . . are lost in admiration of their own bril-
liant originality."[2]

Notes

1. "Dictionary of Literary Biography," Bookrags, http://www.bookrags.com/biog-raphy/w-l-george-dlb (accessed December 31, 2008).
2. Louise Maunsell Field, review of *Ursula Trent* by W. L. George, *New York Times*, October 9, 1921, http://query.nytimes.com/mem/archive-free/pdf?_r=1&res=9E0CE7D71439E133A2575AC0A9669D946095D6CF (accessed December 31, 2008).

Why Condemn? W. L. George Noted English Novelist Asks.

W. L. George, noted English novelist, comes to the defense of the flapper. This keen analyst of feminine psychology presents the case of the ultra-modern girl who so often is condemned because, perhaps, it is almost as much of a fad to condemn her as it is to be a flapper.

It is one of the curiosities of life that the very young should prove irritating to the old. It is as if a wise parent were to look upon his child to see what he should avoid, says Mr. W. L. George.

There is about the young a boldness, a loudness, which irritates those whose years aspire to quiet; they pronounce the words "modern girl" with horror, the word "flapper" with contempt. It seems a pity to me. I love the bright, laughing, high-heeled, low-bloused little animal some call a flapper. That nice child is the first proof of the future woman, and we have no right to complain if this earliest specimen appears rather heavily inked and smudgy at the edges.

Some Are Born Flappers

Besides, flapping is not a matter of age; some of us are born flappers; others at 16 have in them no flap at all. We all know flappers of 40, and we know them as little as we can, for it is sad when the hashed mutton of maturity garnishes itself with the frivolous parsley of youth.

The true flapper begins before she leaves school. Eventually she marries and flaps only with the home—that is, if she is wise. Thus it is the unmarried flapper who interests us; she seems to have so good a time, visiting in one day four restaurants, two theaters and three movies, attending always by an ever-changing man. And yet—the world does cruel things to flappers!

In *Ursula Trent*, I drew the picture of a flapper. She liked pleasure, and she liked men. Being poor, she could get only what men gave her. So men took. If Ursula had not been brave enough to bear all things, she would have been unfit to dare all things; she would not have survived a life of misery and toiling coming at last upon marriage and happiness, knowing herself and her own strength.

That is perhaps the story of many of the flappers we laugh at. In many of them lies tragedy, loveliness, poverty, unrealized ambition, despised love, inability to love. I suggest that a kindlier eye should be allowed to rest on the flapper as she struts along the Great White Way.

Source: *Daily Democrat-Tribune* 45, no. 206, Jefferson City, Missouri, January 10, 1922, front page.

2. Social Results of Alcohol as a Beverage

In 1924 Lamar T. Beman published Selected Articles on Prohibition: Modification of the Volstead Law, *a book that was part of a series for debaters.*[1] *This book contains essays and book and article excerpts that focused on the topic of Prohibition, both pro and con. When this book was released, Prohibition had been in effect for four years. In the introduction to the book, Beman states that four years was not enough time to clearly see how effective the Volstead Act was in eliminating alcohol consumption in the United States.*

Moreover, he points out, "people, with a few exceptions, will watch the workings of a new law that makes a great national experiment and see the results as wholly beneficial or entirely harmful according to their preconceived opinions. Most people will first consider where their personal or financial interest lies, then shape their opinions and arguments on great national issues so as to support their interests, and finally in the operation of a new law be able to see only such results as they want to see, such as conform to their preconceived notions."

The essays reprinted here, "The Monarch of All Human Vices" by Senator Lawrence Y. Sherman, and "The Sum of All Villainies" by Robert G. Ingersoll, were chosen because of the two authors' passionate arguments in favor of Prohibition. They paint a clear picture of how shocking the behavior of some flappers would have been perceived to be in an era when alcohol consumption was illegal and when a significant percentage of Americans did not approve of behavior by women that was perceived as forward and/or immoral.

Note

1. Harry Gene Levine, et al., *Alcohol Control, Particularly Before and at Repeal, A Selected Bibliography,* 1977, Drug Policy Alliance, http://www.lindesmith.org/library/bibliography/alcohol/index.cfm (accessed December 31, 2008).

The Monarch of All Human Vices

Drunkenness is the monarch of all human vices. Other evils are its mere satellites. It permeates and poisons and rots every department of life and every avenue and faculty of the human body. Once in a distant age intoxicating liquor was the supposed instrument of fellowship and good cheer. It is now the debased and adulterated instrument for the exploitation for profit and the promotion of personal vices. It has grown to astounding proportions. The longer it continues, the greater its evil and the more potent its strength. It has entrenched itself with human avarice and become its ally to exploit the pitiable weakness of humanity to accumulate fortunes. The men who have made it their instrument of pecuniary gain have assumed to control political parties, to threaten candidates, to decide elections, to administer civil government, to make new laws, to promote profitable evils and contemptuously to break existing laws they cannot repeal.

The liquor interests have written their own indictment, and accumulated the evidence justifying their own extinction. The breweries have been asked for years to cease to promote the disreputable and irresponsible saloon keeper. They have been asked to clean up the vicious resorts that have been a bane and a menace to decent communities. Their reply was a sneer and the statement that it was the brewer's business to make and sell beer. Whisky has been denounced as a dangerous beverage and restraints demanded for more than half a century.

The answer has been opposition or abuse of those who would regulate as well as those who would prohibit. All who have asked that present laws be obeyed have been stigmatized as fanatics, and fresh infractions of regulatory laws have followed every effort for their enforcement. Wine growers have been advised of the evils gathering about their heads. They, too, have been deaf to the developing hostilities of this generation to intoxicating liquor. If they are caught in the whirlpool of an aroused and righteous indignation, they will but suffer the penalty resulting from their indifference or open sympathy with the more culpable of their kind. A business whose system is lawlessness and whose finished product is a drunkard ought to have no lawful abiding place in this republic. It is an outlaw measured its practices, and a criminal tested by its results. A business that will not be regulated by law must at last be destroyed by law. The traffic in intoxicating liquor has refused to be regulated, and therefore earned the penalty of legislative extinction. Its promises of reformation are to be weighed in the light of its past performances. The breweries' efforts to reform the saloon keeper are to be measured by their creation of his disreputable kind.

Source: *Congressional Record* 55 (August 1, 1917): 5645–5646. Reprinted from Lamar T. Beman, comp., *Selected Articles on Prohibition: Modification of the Volstead Law* (New York: H. W. Wilson, 1924), 53–56.

The Sum of all Villainies

I am aware that there is a prejudice against any man who manufactures alcohol. I believe that from the time it issues from the coiled and poisonous worms in the distillery until it empties into the jaws of death, dishonor and crime, it demoralizes everybody that touches it, from its source to where it ends. I do not believe anybody can contemplate the object without being prejudiced against the liquor crime.

All we have to do is to think of the wrecks on either bank of the stream of death, of the suicides, of the insanity, of the ignorance, of the destitution, of the little children tugging at the faded and withered breast of weeping and despairing mothers, of wives asking for bread, of the men of genius it has wrecked, the men struggling with imaginary serpents, produced by this devilish thing; and when you think of the jails, of the almshouses, of the asylums, of the prisons, of the scaffolds upon either bank, I do not wonder that every thoughtful man is prejudiced against this damned stuff called alcohol. Intemperance cuts downs youth in its vigor, manhood in its strength, old age in its weakness. It breaks a father's heart, bereaves the doting mother, extinguishes natural affection, erases conjugal love, blots out filial attachment, blights parental hopes, brings down mourning age in sorrow to the grave. It produces weakness, not life. It makes wives widows; children orphans; fathers fiends, and all of them paupers and beggars. It feeds rheumatism, invites cholera, imports pestilence and embraces consumption. It covers the land with idleness, misery, crime. It fills your jails, supplies your almshouses and demands your asylums. It engenders controversies, fosters quarrels and cherishes riots.

It crowds your penitentiaries and furnishes victims for your scaffold. It is the life blood of the gambler, the element of the burglar, the prop of the highwayman and support of the midnight incendiary. It countenances the liar, respects the thief, esteems the blasphemer. It violates obligation, reverences fraud and honors infamy. It defames benevolence, hates love, scorns virtue and slanders innocence. It incites the father to butcher his helpless offspring, helps the husband to massacre his wife and the child to grind the patricidal ax. It burns up men, consumes women, detests life, curses God, despises heaven. It suborns witnesses, nurses perjury, defiles the jury box and stains judicial ermine. It degrades the citizen, debases the legislator, dishonors the statesman and disarms the patriot. It brings shame, not honor; misery, not safety; despair, not hope; misery, not happiness, and with the malevolence of a fiend it calmly surveys its frightful desolation and unsatiated havoc. It poisons felicity, kills peace, ruins morals, blights confidence, slays reputations, and wipes out national honor, then curses the world and laughs at its ruin. It does all that and more. It murders the soul. It is the sum of all villainies, the father of all crimes, the mother of all abominations, the devil's best friend and God's worst enemy.

Source: *Commoner* 13 (July 11, 1913): 13. Reprinted from Lamar T. Beman, comp., *Selected Articles on Prohibition: Modification of the Volstead Law* (New York: H. W. Wilson, 1924), 53–56.

3. Death Blow to the Flapper

This piece appeared in the Daily Democrat-Tribune *on July 20, 1922, and, by reading the text, you can actually feel the smoldering rage that the writer, Hedda Hoyt, must have felt when merely mentioning the word "flappers"—and the spiteful triumph that she must have felt when she (erroneously) announced that women will begin wearing long skirts again. There are a number of spelling mistakes within this piece; perhaps Hoyt, like my neighbor, gets a case of the "flying fingers" when writing about something infuriating—but you have to wonder about the editing/proof-reading staff who was working that day at the newspaper.*

Although this appears as one article, it reads more like a series of three articles, broken up by bolded subheadings. The first one is Hoyt's announce-ment that flappers are going to be tossed to the "junk heap of forgotten pasts" and apparently they are also going to give their "low-heeled sandals" to the "household cook"; the second is an unnamed French connoisseur's opinion that American women dress better on the streets than when in "smart restaurants and roof gardens"; and the third is Hoyt's advice as to how women, from "shop girls" to women whose names appear on the "social register" can add class to their wardrobe and overall appearance.

Long Skirts Mean That the Saucy, Little Bobbed Head Must Go

In accordance with the evolution of dress, flappers are destined to be relagated [*sic*] to the junk heap of forgotten pasts.

The little knee-length skirts and saucy hats are doomed to rest in the garret with the hoop skirts and bonnets of other days.

The same bobbed head-dress is to receive the same fate of the spit curls of yester-year. The household cook is to fall heir to the low-heeled sandals.

And the culprit who wished all of this on us is—the long skirt. There is no use arguing about it, the long skirt is coming back. Some joykillers say is it here already.

"What does the long skirt have to do with ousting the flapper?" you ask. "Can you imagine a long-skirted female with a crop of short hair? It can't be done."

The little bobbed heads simply demanded the bobbed skirts and now with skirts r[e]aching within four inch[e]s of the floor, the flapper is certainly undergoing "one of the crises" of her life.

Taste in Dinner Frocks

"American women are better dressed on the streets than when in smart restaurants and roof gardens," commented a French connoisseaur [*sic*] of gowns who returned to Paris this week.

"It is surprising," he said, "to note the difference between the excellent taste of American street costumes and the lack of taste in dinner frocks. On the Avenue, one finds little distinction between the shop girl and the debutante. They are all beautifully shod; their gowns have the chic of French creations; their bearing reminds one of the ancient Greeks and their figures are superb. But," he added, "they could learn the art of dressing for the dinner hours and for the roof gardens from the European women. In America there is either too much over dressing or too much under-dressing at informal gatherings."

Those of us who resent foreign criticism of American women's dress will do well to glance about us at the smart restaurants. If the edbutante [*sic*] is usually too overpoweringly gowned in evening frocks that should be worn exclusively at formal functions. The shop girl with the out-of-town buyer is either gowned in a home-made replica of the gown of the debutante or in a street dress with a street hat. The flapper flaps at the dinner hour just as she has flapped all day—fringed skirt, woolen hose, sweater and a sport hat flopping over one eye.

In a room of two hundred women, perhaps only thirty will be appropriately gowned. We are an odd mixture of weeds and orchids.

At public places, where anyone who has the price of a dinner may congregate, there should be the semi-evening frock. There should not be cut too extreme in décolleté and should have some semblance of sleeves.

Advice to Flappers

The flapper should [get] out of her flapper aiment [*sic*] at the dinner hours into a pretty colorful georgette. She can look just as girlish in a little snug-fitting bodice with tiny puffed sleeves and a full, fluffy skirt as [she] can in knee-length plaids which are only suitable for sport or day wear.

The shop girl will find a mauve or dull hued crepe de chene [*sic*] suitable for dinner wear and one which will come within the bounds of her pocketbook. By selecting georgette in neutral shades which are so popular just now, she may add different colored slips and sashes and feel that she has an entirely new frock.

The same suggestion can be used with the Spanish lace gowns that are having such a vouge [*sic*] at present. A mauve colored lace frock cut on long waisted lines, with wide flowing lace sleeves and uneven hem line, may be worn over salmon yellow, orchid, orange or any pastel shade that is becoming. By changing the underslip, the whole gown is changed.

The underslip for these above mentioned gowns need not be of silk, for the lingette [*sic*] material is fully as soft and is far less expensive.

One can not tell the woman with her name on the social register how she should dress in public places, but her breeding and good taste should tell her that too much elaboration is not the thing.

Source: Hedda Hoyt, *Daily Democrat-Tribune* 46, no. 4 (July 20, 1922).

4. Flappers 4,000 Years Ago!

If you believe that there are truly no new ideas under the sun, then you'll heartily agree with this short piece of whimsical writing that was published in the Daily Democrat-Tribune *on April 22, 1922. Although the tone is lighthearted, the writer is summarizing information from a long-standing research organization that still exists, providing serious scholarship, even today: the American Oriental Society.*

According to their Web site (http://www.umich.edu/~aos), the American Oriental Society is the "oldest learned society in the United States devoted to a particular field of scholarship"—in this case, the works of humans in Asia.

Founded in 1842, the society originally focused on research into the languages and literatures of Asia and has since expanded to include "philology, literary criticism, textual criticism, paleography, epigraphy, linguistics, biography, archaeology, and the history of the intellectual and imaginative aspects of Oriental civilizations, especially of philosophy, religion, folklore and art." They publish the Journal of the American Oriental Society, *with today's editor-in-chief from the University of Colorado, and the associate editors from the University of Michigan, the University of California–Los Angeles, and Harvard Law School.*

Enjoy! This piece is just plain fun to read.

Modern Girl Merely "Stealing Stuff" from Stone Age

The flapper and her fuzzy chinned puddle jumping lover of four thousand years ago—ah, there is something to get excited about. They invented love making.

Modern juvenile cut-ups, whose alleged shamelessness has caused outraged shrieks from certain quarters—there isn't a new idea in a million of them, in the opinion of the distinguished membership of the American Oriental Society.

Flappers are stealing their stuff from snappy and pictured articles by "advanced" authors written on bricks and tablets when Babylonia was so young that chambers of commerce were ballyhooing it as a coining nation and a fine place to settle.

Bobs and Short Ones

Speakers before the society today showed flappers pictured on bricks four thousand years old. They pointed out the bobbed hair, the short skirts, the sandals, the plucked eyebrows. They remarked how the goggle-eyed youth of the day resembled our own puddle jumpers. They read the "hot stuff" inscriptions beneath the pictured flappers. Some of it was slang. The girls had love codes, and spent much time parading up and down the Nile promenades wearing their vampish earrings; Outraged fathers wrote on imperishable stone what a nuisance the young bloods were and what was the world coming to with girls and boys out on the Euphrates in boats at all hours, singing "popular" songs while strumming the ukuleles of that vintage.

Source: *Daily Democrat-Tribune* 45, no. 294 (April 22, 1922).

5. "Fatty" Arbuckle Denies Guilt in His Testimony

Roscoe "Fatty" Arbuckle wasn't your typical movie star, being significantly overweight. In 1909, though, he began performing in Hollywood; shortly after that, he was frequently a Keystone Cop in Mack Sennett's productions. By 1913, he was costarring in pictures with Mabel Normand and, by 1917, Arbuckle had complete creative control over his films, so he hired a young unknown named Buster Keaton—which led to even more successes. Arbuckle was most likely the first Hollywood actor who was paid $1 million annually.[1] Unfortunately, just a few short years later, all went dreadfully wrong for Arbuckle.

On September 3, 1921, in the St. Francis Hotel in San Francisco, there was a wild party being held in Arbuckle's room. During the party, an actress named Virginia Rappe became ill and, several days later, died of peritonitis triggered by a ruptured bladder. A friend of Rappe's demanded that Arbuckle be charged with raping Virginia Rappe and, through that action, causing her painful death. Stories of how Arbuckle allegedly caused this injury ranged from a rape by a beer bottle or a champagne bottle—or by Arbuckle crushing her with his massive weight.

When Arbuckle was brought to trial, Rappe's friend who had insisted upon charges being filed did not testify because of her record, which included extortion, racketeering, and bigamy.

Needless to say, the country was spellbound by the peek into the wild lives of Hollywood stars and starlets and at the lurid accusations pointing to Arbuckle. Both newspaper reporters and groups espousing moral living harassed Arbuckle, who denied all charges. According to Arbuckle, he had found Rappe in a bathroom, vomiting and moaning in pain, so he helped her to a bed, where he left her.

During the time of the accusation and trials, Arbuckle's movies were banned in both America and Britain. The site of Virginia Rappe's grave is alleged to be haunted.

Note

1. Howard Chua-Eoan, "Top 25 Crimes of the Century: The Fatty Arbuckle Scandal, 1920," n.d., http://www.time.com/time/2007/crimes/4.html (accessed January 1, 2009).

Arbuckle Tells of Events in His Room from Witness Stand

Film Comedian Denies He Inflicted Injuries on Miss Rappe Causing Her Death.
Found Her Moaning With Pain in Bathroom
Did Not Place Ice on Woman's Body Following Party, He Says.

Roscoe Arbuckle, motion comedian, spoke today in a tragic drama of which he has been the central figure since its inception September 5, last. Arbuckle told from the witness stand his own story of the happenings of a party in his room at the Hotel St. Francis here which preceded by a few days the death of Virginia Rappe, one of those who attended.

It was at this party that the girl received injuries which caused her death, the prosecution contends, and it is that allegation that forms the basis of Arbuckle's trial, now drawing to a close, on the charge of manslaughter.

The defense closed its case late today and tomorrow the prosecution will commence its presentation of rebuttal testimony. The case is expected to go to the jury Thursday.

Arbuckle denied that he inflicted the injuries on Miss Rappe that have been charged against him.

"When I went during the party to dress for an engagement I had with a friend, I found Miss Rappe on the bathroom floor writhing and moaning," he said. "When I opened the door of the bathroom it struck against her. I assisted her in the bathroom all I could, then I placed her on the bed in my room and continued to assist her."

Arbuckle said he did not know that the party had been planned and that he did not know that it had become a reality until Miss Prevost, Miss Rappe and other guests arrived.

He denied the truth of statements reported to have been made by him following the party that he placed a piece of ice on Miss Rappe's body. Hundreds of persons rushed the court room doors when Arbuckle was on the stand, trying to gain admission. The court officers, the attendants and counsels had great difficulty in getting to their places.

The defense offered the deposition of Dr. H. M. Resenberg of Chicago, which said that in 1918 he treated Miss Rappe for a bladder ailment. Miss Rappe died from a ruptured bladder, said by the prosecution to have been caused by external force applied by Arbuckle. The defense alleges that the injuries resulted from a chronic condition. The deposition was allowed by the court.

Source: *Daily Capital News*, November 29, 1921, front page.

6. "Fatty" Arbuckle Acquitted by Jury in His Third Trial

Roscoe "Fatty" Arbuckle, who was charged with the manslaughter of starlet Virginia Rappe, endured three criminal trials. The first trial ended with a hung jury, with a 10 to 2 vote for acquittal; at the second trial, the inverse occurred, with the hung jury voting 10 to 2 for conviction. It should be noted that Arbuckle testified in his defense in the first trial, but not in the second. So, when it was time for the third trial to begin, the defense team decided that Arbuckle's testimony was persuasive, so once again he testified in his own defense. In the third trial, Arbuckle was acquitted, with the jury feeling a need to apologize to him for all that he had suffered through the justice system.

Arbuckle was briefly blacklisted from filmmaking; even after the ban was lifted, he struggled to find work in Hollywood. Finally, Buster Keaton—one of the few people who did not abandon Arbuckle after the Virginia Rappe debacle—suggested that Arbuckle take on the pseudonym of Will B. Good and then work behind the scenes on films. Arbuckle took him up on his suggestion, using the name William B. Goodrich. Using that name, he did find some work.

On June 29, 1933, after celebrating his one-year anniversary with his third wife, Arbuckle suffered a fatal heart attack in the night. Here's a contemporary look at his third trial, one that should have cleared his name, but never really did.

Verdict Exonerates Movie Actor of Manslaughter Charge in Death of Virginia Rappe—Comedian Has No Plans for Immediate Future

Jurors Issue Statement Declaring "Great Injustice Has Been Done" Arbuckle

A verdict of acquittal was returned by a jury today in the third trial of Roscoe "Fatty" Arbuckle on a manslaughter charge growing out of the death of Miss Virginia Rappe, motion picture actress. The jury was out six minutes.

Edward Brown, whose presence in the jury was objected to by the prosecution, was foreman.

The defendant was deeply affected, the verdict being received by him with a great sigh of relief. There was no demonstration, the court having warned against it.

Mrs. Minta Arbuckle, the defendant's wife, cried quietly. Both she and Arbuckle shook hands with the jury.

The quick return of the jury was a surprise. The verdict was by acclamation, the deliberation taking less time than a minute. Additional time was consumed by detail. The jurors and spectators crowded by Arbuckle and his counsel and finally bore him off the jury room to congratulations.

"Arbuckle has no immediate plans," Gavin McNab, his chief counsel, said. "It was a splendid verdict."

"The jury did its duty," was the verdict of Milton Uren, assistant attorney.

Mrs. Arbuckle expressed her thanks to McNab by giving him a resounding kiss. The jury held an informal reception with Arbuckle in the jury room.

A group of jurors headed by Brown issued a statement which said: "Acquittal is not enough for Arbuckle. We feel a great injustice has been done him. He acted in a manly manner and told a straightforward story."

Source: *Daily Capital News*, April 13, 1922, front page.

7. The Fable of the Flapper

On August 13, 1922, the Mansfield News *from Mansfield, Ohio, published interviews with several young females who in some way identified with the flapper label. The compilation, titled "The Fable of the Flapper," is a lengthy article, with about two-thirds of the text reprinted here.*

The anonymous writer who created this story seems in one way to be quite liberal and open-minded, defending the females who consider themselves flappers. Her tone is that of an indulgent aunt clucking over the young'uns and wheedling the stern parents to simply look the other way to let the darlings have some fun. The message, though, is more mixed than that. The writer is not as understanding of women past their teen years who indulge in "flapperism," using phrases such as "old-style vamp" and "rather disgusting" to describe them.

Moreover, the ending of the article, which is not included in the portion of the article reprinted below, adds yet another twist to this writer's philosophy. In the closing text, the writer reassures readers who might be nervously biting their nails at the notion of giving open-ended approval and freedoms to girls who admit to enjoying a good time that the flapper is merely "storing up wisdom for the time when she meets her Prince Charming . . . having made up her mind she will have more of a chance even than the Princess in the fairy tale of 'living happily ever afterwards.'"

Once upon a time a woman reporter became mighty curious to "know if flappers really are. Well—er. Naughty as they are painted." So she selected a number of flappers who were typical of the prevailing flapper type and interviewed 'em.

And right away she was immensely surprised. She didn't expect 'em to be bad, oh no. But she did think they might be very indiscreet, perhaps. But the only one who had done foolish things admitted that it didn't pay.

Just remember that the reporter did not talk to girls whom she knew to be of questionable character, but instead she selected those about whose flapperism there might be a bit of a question. And as far as she was concerned she became convinced that the word "flapper" means nothing worse than youthful freedom and the expression of vivid personality.

There were several things she decided after a few interviews and the first is that flapperism stands for lively, up-to-the-minute girlhood of a lassie in her teens, who likes above everything else a good time. She has a mind of her own, she loves to do the things that are progressive and she thinks, which is one reason she does have a decisive intelligence.

Furthermore, she discovered that there are many women who are parading in the apparel of the flappers who are not entitled to the name. That they are simply old-style vamp, disguised in an habiliment [*sic*] that should typify only the girl not yet out of her teens. She is the one who has done all the harm for the real flappers. In other words, she is an illustration of the parable of the "wolf in sheep's clothing." That may be rather a strong statement, but that all the high ideals that characterize a good woman should imitate the one word that means essentially "youth" when their youth has been left behind long ago, is rather disgusting. The word flapper is supposed to have originated from mediaeval time when the name was given to a young girl because of her "flappy" habits, much resembling a young duck. Surely, no one accused a duckling of being bad.

And now for the interviews. One girl talked with is one of the best known girls in Mansfield. She is peppy, full of life and a typical flapper. Wears knicker dresses, bobbed hair and is essentially vivacious. Yet it was discovered that she has the finest of ideals and ideas. Asked what her opinion of a flapper is she said: "I think a flapper is a girl who likes to do things. She likes to play tennis, golf, go swimming, ride horseback and all the things there are to do. She wears knicker clothes and bobs her hair because they are comfortable, and because she can do more things when dressed that way. I think that flappers have been abused for they are not bad; they are simply modern.

Personally, I love to do things. I have lived in the city all my life and never saw a cow until I was nine years old. Now, when I get a chance to get out of doors, I just play with all my might. I love to read, especially all about outdoor life and then for a change, I bring out Poe's work. My mother and I are regular chums. I have a wonderful mother. There are just she and I, and almost everywhere I go she goes along."

And all the time she was talking, she used an almost perfect vocabulary for so young a person. No girl who is utterly careless and thoughtless would have stored in her mind such a choice of words to express her thoughts. And no girl who thinks of her mother as she did, even though she is a flapper and may do foolish things once in a while, is a daughter of whom anyone needs to be ashamed.

Another girl of the flapper type, but who is a trifle older than the others, has "flapped" with a bit of indiscretion. But her "flapping" days are over and she is ready to settle down.

"I am to be married," she said, "and my biggest ambition just now is to have a home and a baby. For the past three years, I have had a good time and found there was nothing to it. Any girl who dances every night, who goes out on auto parties, would not do those things if she stopped to think, but she doesn't so she has a good time."

The question, "Do you consider yourself a flapper?" was asked, and she answered:

"If bobbed hair is typical of the flapper, I suppose I am. But I am not sorry I bobbed my hair and I am not going to get married until it grows out longer. Married women should not be flappers."

There you have it again. Women out of their teens should not ape flapperism, because the day will come when they want to consider marriage and flapper styles are not suitable to married woman.

Another popular Mansfield girl who has hair typical, whose clothes are always in the latest mode, and who was graduated last year from high school, voices the flapper idea thus:

"I love to have a good time in the right way. Although I sometimes wish I had not started having a good time so soon because now everything is the same; there is nothing new. But I love to dance and go to parties. Mother doesn't allow me to go auto riding for she says that I have a home and if I entertain company, I must do it there."

Do you think girls think of other things today besides having a good time?

"Yes, I do. There are hardly any girls who graduated with me who are not working some place, and like their work immensely."

"How does the idea of making a home appeal to you?"

"I think it is fine, but personally I don't think I would make a very good home-maker. Business appeals to me more. My own home life is fine, though, and we have the jolliest time."

8. In Mary's Eyes

Mary Pickford and Douglas Fairbanks were huge film stars when this article was written in 1922. Mary was known as "America's Sweetheart" and "Little Mary" and their sprawling mansion was known as "Pickfair." In this New York Times *interview, the writer—Benjamin De Casseres— seems quite star struck by Pickford, calling her "Princess" and "Princess Mary," while shortening her husband's name to just plain "Doug."*

De Casseres romanticized their relationship, writing the following: "I glimpsed an incarnation of the end of every man's and woman's desire— the Perfect Couple. They were Romance, Love, Youth. No wonder Paris and London followed them with shouts and flowers! Strength has taken unto itself a bride called Beauty."

Only a portion of the article, "In Mary's Eyes," is reprinted here, which is the section titled "Flappers of All Kinds," along with a very small segment of the next section, which is titled "Be Careful!" Although the reprinted section was apparently to focus on flappers, the subject is quickly changed so that Pickford could focus on what cynical critics would suggest was her favorite topic: Mary Pickford.

The couple did contribute much to the development of Hollywood, with Fairbanks, Pickford, director D. W. Griffith, and silent-film comedian Charlie Chaplin creating United Artists in 1919 so that they could distribute their own films; this was unheard of and it changed the way that the film industry was run.

By the end of the 1920s, Fairbanks and Pickford's popularity was waning, so in 1929 they starred in a film together: The Taming of the Shrew. *The film did not do well and, in 1933, they retired. In 1936 the couple divorced, with Fairbanks quickly marrying his mistress, Lady Sylvia Ashley. In 1937 Pickford married actor and musician Charles "Buddy" Rogers and they adopted two children.*

Miss Pickford's Views on Flappers, Here and in Europe—Hollywood—Screen and Real Life "Doug's Running Comment"

Flappers of All Kinds

"Talking about flappers," said Mary. "I have met all kinds in all sorts of big cities. They think they are meeting me while in reality I am meeting them. I put them on the screen—a bit here and a bit there; but they do not know it."

"Your life," advanced Doug, "is just one subtle psychic observation after another."

"Something like that," said Mary, "although it is too early in the morning for such wise observations. Psychology should come after the coffee in the evening."

"I found the flappers of London and Paris poorly gowned—"

"Dressed," cut in Doug.

"Gowned, I said," said Mary positively. "Maybe it is the result of the war or something—"

"Do you think the mark, the franc and the pound will ever come back?" interrupted Doug.

"—or something," went on Mary, paying no attention to her mate. "When it comes to women—flappers or otherwise—I must stick to the U.S.A. After my trip abroad I found that our women were the most charming, the most beautiful and the best dressed of them all. But I must say this, that on the Continent of Europe I found people generally more sincere than they are here. They think less of personal peccadilloes over there than we do here. Probably our charm lies in this art of camouflage [*sic*], these beautiful little hypocrisies, these—"

"Philosophy as well as psychology, then, over the dinner coffee, dear Mary," came back Doug, as he whirled a ring of smoke out the window toward a traffic cop.

"Is it true," I asked, "that Mr. Fairbanks selects your clothes?"

Doug looked esoterically at the roof of the car. Mary rippled out a laugh. I felt as though I had opened my mouth and put my foot in it.

"No," said Mary. "Of course not. How did ever such an absurd thing enter your head? As a matter of fact, I select his clothes, for—"

"Only my ties, dear, not my clothes," came from Doug, half plaintively.

"Ties, then," conceded Mary, in order probably to keep peace in the family. "He buys—when loose—the most extraordinary ties that were ever conceived in a cubist's brain. That is, he did until I gave them all to Bill Hart and bought him a lot that were subdued.

"I suppose that story that Mr. Fairbanks selected my clothes got around from the fact that he insists that I dress plainly, simply and untheatrically. But as I always did, you see he is not entitled to the credit he gets for that—is he?"

"Mary," said Doug," do you remember what Mark Twain said was his highest ambition in life?"

"No," replied Mary, "but that's your usual way of dodging me. Well, what was Mr. Twain's greatest ambition in life?"

"To throw a raw egg into a revolving electric fan in a public restaurant."

"Whatever put that in your head?" I asked.

"A man just passed up Fifth Avenue with long whiskers, and I never see such an ornament that I do not want to set it on fire. Now Freud would say—"

"Oh, my favorite hobby?" crosswired Mary. "I have three—work, my brother Jack and Good Cheer. Maybe Good Cheer is my real hobby. Laugh at Pollyanna if you will—I believe in her as I believe in every part I have ever played. Satirize Keep Smiling all who will—it keeps the world sane.

"I love old people as well as young—and I do all I can in my little way to keep them cheerful and smiling. You see, I am a very simple, ordinary woman, and I haven't anything of that Cosmic stuff in my makeup. Einstein—"

"Izzy or the other nuisance?" asked Doug.

"No," pursued Mary, "I do not care anything about those Einsteins."

"Did you know that I am going to direct Jack, my brother, in his next picture?"

"Megaphone—and all that?" asked Doug, smiling the smile of male credulity.

"Megaphone and everything!" shouted Mary, clapping her hands in childish glee. "I shall be Director Mary Pickford—wait and see!"

And then from gay to grave:

"I would not act a role that I did not believe in—did not love. I am literally the parts I play. They are parts of myself—that is Mary Pickford. I believe that is the secret of art—of all art. An artist's life and an artist's work should be complementary. If an actor's role is not part and parcel of himself or herself, it will not 'get over.' I have succeeded because I have put heart and soul into my creations. What I am not personally I can not depict. Nor would the public stand for it. And they are right.

"Fame?—I never think of it. Maybe that's the reason it's so busy with me. Of course I enjoy being famous, but it is the most inconvenient thing—sometimes—in the world. . . .

[*Section of dialogue between Douglas Fairbanks and the reporter is not reproduced here.*]

"I cannot conceive myself out of pictures. It is like asking Alice to leave Wonderland or Titania the magic woods. We screen phantoms, you know—lead a double life."

"Be Careful!"

"Mary! Mary!" exploded Doug. "Be careful—he's a reporter!"

"A double life, as I said," went on the Princess, "but what Doug would call, psychologically speaking. There is myself, you know, as you see me here, and my other self in phantom-land. I shall never forget the crash in my soul when I first saw myself on the screen. I thought I had died and gone to ghostland. It was some time before I could look at myself again."

Source: Benjamin De Casseres, "In Mary's Eyes," *New York Times,* March 5, 1922.

9. Queens of Film Colony Face Grilling in Taylor Murder Probe

On February 9, 1922, California's Oakland Tribune *published multiple articles about the murder of Hollywood director William Desmond Taylor, which had occurred some time late on February 1. This murder captured the attention of people all across the country, especially when some of the most beautiful actresses of the day, especially Mabel Normand, were implicated, rightly or wrongly, in this dark tale.*

Sensational theories abounded, with one of them reprinted here: that police suspected the murder to be modeled after a scene in one of Taylor's films, with one of the actresses involved in the films potentially also involved in this death. It was sincerely hoped that a "clew" could be found to support this theory.

This murder case was never solved, although there were deathbed confessions decades later. From 1993 to 2000, Bruce Long of Arizona State University gathered and transcribed hundreds of articles connected to Taylor and/or about people suspected of murdering him. Several issues of this journal, Taylorology, *are available online at http://www.taylorology. com, and a note on that site indicates that more issues will be added. This journal is also a rich source of information about other well-known Hollywood stars of the era.*

As noted in an article reprinted here, the district attorney handed off the prosecution of suspected murderer Madalynne Obenchain to focus on the Taylor shooting. Prior to the Taylor death, the Obenchain case had garnered significant attention, as Madalynne Obenchain was considered quite beautiful and it was said that all she needed to do was wink at a man to get her way.[1]

Obenchain had left her husband, an attorney, so that she could be with John Belton Kennedy; when Kennedy was killed with Obenchain nearby,

she was accused of murder and was put on trial five times; after five hung
juries, the prosecutor declined to try her again.

Now, back to Taylor:

Note

1. Tessa Sandstrom, "A Hollywood Murder, Part 2," October 18, 2006, http://
   www.prairiepublic.org/programs/datebook/bydate/06/1006/101806.jsp
   (accessed January 12, 2009).

Woolwine Drops Obenchain Case for Film Death

District Attorney Takes Full Charge of Investigation in Taylor Case

District Attorney Thomas Lee Woolwine, it was announced today, has turned the case of Madalynne Obenchain, on trial for murder, over to his chief deputy and devoted his attention to the murder of William Desmond Taylor, film director. Complex angles of acts that occurred since the murder itself were placed under exhaustive scrutiny.

They include recovery of a packet of letters, including some written by Mabel Normand, actress, and the last person known to the police to have been with Taylor just prior to his death. It was announced at the district attorney's office that these letters would not be made public at this time.

The centralized investigation will be carried on as follows:

Questioning of two men, not connected with motion pictures, along lines of "jealousy" as a motive in the case.

Close examination of former employees of the slain director in order to reveal intimacies of the past that came under their observation. Among those who will figure in the investigation are Mabel Normand, Mary Miles Minter, Neva Gerber and Claire Windsor, motion picture actresses, the first three of whom have been reported to have been parties to love affairs with Taylor; Henry Peavey, negro houseman, who found the body; Howard Fellows, former chauffeur of Taylor; Charles Eyton, manager of the Famous Players-Laskey Studios, in which Taylor was employed; Mrs. Douglas MacLean, neighbor of Taylor, who saw a stranger leaving the Taylor doorway after hearing a shot there on the night of the murder, and a host of others.

Murder Planned After Film Plot, Is Police View

Picture Catalogues Checked Up for Similar "Tragedies" Before Camera

Several times within the past few years the screens have flashed before thrill-hardened audiences a suggestion for crime which fits, as a hand in a glove, into the latest theory of the Taylor murder. The catalogs of the movies today are being turned back, all of these scenes are being checked and the actors and actresses who took part in them are listed for an intensive study of possibilities.

The scene?

Here's Movie Scene

A girl, desperate, leading a man to his death. With a glint in her eyes all but buried beneath a surface glance of allurement, she smiles and backs slowly, beckoning, provocative. The villain, for it is generally the villain who meets this end in the films, gathers the girl in his arms. She smiles at him, then turning to the audience registers horror and hate. In her hand she holds behind his back a small revolver . . .

This scene, in its main outline, has been thrown before motion picture crowds at least three times in the last 18 months. Twice, it was a revolver, and once a knife, but always the man held the girl in his arms and met death while she smiled at him.

Theory in D.A. Case

The theory in the Taylor case is that such a scene was enacted in life. Certain it is the revolver was held close to the back of the director and that his arms were partly raised. Could it have been, the investigators are asking, that one of the women of the screen who had rehearsed before the camera (even under Taylor's direction) such a scene had turned to its suggestion when desperation had seized upon her brain and soul?

In the chance that a clew may be picked up, the films of the past two years are being gone over. Scenes similar to that built up in police theory will be given careful attention and the women who have taken part in them will be checked with the women whose names have, so far, been brought in the case.

Miss Normand Due at Work Tomorrow

Mabel Normand, who has been under care of specialists since her collapse at the funeral of William D. Taylor, is much improved today and will be ready to testify with other of Taylor's friends before District Attorney Woolwine if she is requested, the Mack Sennett studios announced.

The call board of the big Glendale boulevard comedy shop today posted Miss Normand's company to resume work tomorrow morning.

The Normand company, directed by F. Richard Jones, is making "Suzanna," a Spanish romance of California, in 1835. Work on the picture has been suspended since the Taylor tragedy.

Estate Drops Down to $20,000

Public Administrator Bryson today let it be known that investigation has shown that the estate of William Desmond Taylor, believed to have amounted to $100,000, has dwindled to $20,000. A large additional sum, however, was believed to be on deposit in a New York bank and efforts today were being made to locate it. Under Taylor's will, his daughter, Ethel Daisy, is the sole beneficiary.

Hundreds of checks found in Taylor's effects showed he had made frequent loans to members of the profession. Endorsement on the checks showed men of much prominence had been aided financially by Taylor. The checks were turned over to the district attorney.

Source: *Oakland Tribune*, February 9, 1922, 6.

Selected Bibliography

Albertson, Chris. *Bessie*. New Haven, CT: Yale University Press, 2005.

Allen, Frederick, L. *Only Yesterday: An Informal History of the 1920s*. New York: Harper Perennial Modern Classics, 2000.

Arnold, Gary. "Silent Siren Out of the Box: DVD Celebrates Louise Brooks." *Washington Times*, February 8, 2007, M21.

Benchley, Robert C. *The Benchley Roundup: A Selection by Nathaniel Benchley of His Favorites*. Chicago: University of Chicago Press, 2001.

Benchley, Robert. *Robert Benchley's Wayward Press: The Complete Collection of His New Yorker Columns Written as Guy Fawkes*. Miami, FL: Wolf Den Books, 2008.

Bengston, John, and Kevin Brownlow. *Silent Traces: Discovering Early Hollywood Through the Films of Charlie Chaplin*. Santa Monica, CA: Santa Monica Press, 2006.

"Bessie Smith." Selected Artist Biography, Jazz: A Film by Ken Burns. PBS. http://www.pbs.org.

Broer, Lawrence R., and John D. Walther. *Dancing Fools and Weary Blues: The Great Escape of the Twenties*. Bowling Green, OH: Bowling Green State University Popular Press, 1990.

Brooks, Louise. *Lulu in Hollywood: Expanded Edition*. Minneapolis: University of Minnesota Press, 2000.

Bruccoli, Matthew Joseph, Scottie Fitzgerald Smith, and Joan Paterson Kerr, eds. The *Romantic Egoists: A Pictorial Autobiography from the Scrapbooks and*

Albums of F. Scott and Zelda Fitzgerald. Columbia: University of South Carolina Press, 2003.

Chandler, Charlotte. *Not the Girl Next Door: Joan Crawford, A Personal Biography*. New York: Applause Books, 2009.

Chaplin, Charlie. *My Autobiography*. New York: Penguin Modern Classics, 2003.

Cohen, Paula Marantz. *Silent Film and the Triumph of the American Myth*. New York: Oxford University Press, 2001.

Drowne, Kathleen. *The 1920s: American Popular Culture Through History*. Westport, CT: Greenwood Press, 2004.

Dumenil, Lynn. *The Modern Temper: American Culture and Society in the 1920s*. New York: Hill and Wang, 1995.

Ellington, Edward Kennedy. *Music Is My Mistress*. New York: Da Capo Press, 1976.

Ellington, Mercer. *Duke Ellington in Person: An Intimate Memoir*. New York: Da Capo Press, 1979.

Fass, Paula S. *The Damned and the Beautiful: American Youth in the 1920s*. New York: Oxford University Press, 2007.

Feinstein, Stephen. *The 1920s from Prohibition to Charles Lindbergh (Decades of the 20th Century in Color)*. Berkeley Heights, NJ: Enslow, 2006.

Feldman, Herman. *Prohibition: Its Economic and Industrial Aspects*. New York: D. Appleton, 1927.

Galewitz, Herb, ed. *Classic Spot Illustrations from the Twenties and Thirties: by James Montgomery Flagg, Gluyas Williams, John Held Jr. et al*. Pictorial Archive Series. New York: Dover Publications, 2000.

Goldberg, David J. *Discontented America: The United States in the 1920s*. Baltimore: Johns Hopkins University Press, 1999.

Gourley, Catherine. *Flappers and the New American Woman: Perceptions of Women from 1918 Through the 1920s*. Images and Issues of Women in the Twentieth Century. Breckenridge, CO: Twenty-First Century Books, 2007.

Hanson, Erica. *A Cultural History of the United States Through the Decades—The 1920s*. A Cultural History of the United States Through the Decades Series. San Diego: Lucent Books, 1998.

Held, John, Jr. *The Works of John Held Jr.* Whitefish, MT: Kessinger, 2007.

Helmer, William J. *St. Valentine's Day Massacre: The Untold Story of the Gangland Bloodbath That Brought Down Al Capone*. Nashville: Cumberland House, 2006.

Huff, Theodore. *Charlie Chaplin*. New York: Henry Schuman, 1951.

Hyland, William G. *George Gershwin: A New Biography*. Westport, CT: Praeger, 2003.

Iorizzo, Luciano. *Al Capone: A Biography*. Westport, CT: Greenwood Press, 2003.

Irwin, Will. "The Greatest Reporter in the World." Iowa Digital Library/University of Iowa [Online January 28, 2009] <http://sdrc.lib.uiowa.edu>.

Kobler, John. *Ardent Spirits: The Rise and Fall of Prohibition*. New York: Da Capo Press, 1993.

Kobler, John. *Capone: The Life and World of Al Capone*. New York: Da Capo Press, 2004.

Latham, Angela J. *Posing a Threat: Flappers, Chorus Girls, and Other Brazen Performers of the American 1920s*. Indianapolis: Wesleyan, 2000.

Lawrence, Jerome, and Robert E. Lee. *Inherit the Wind*. New York: Bantam, 1969.

Lewis, David. *The Portable Harlem Renaissance Reader*. African American History. New York: Penguin, 1995.

Linder, Doug. "John Scopes." University of Missouri–Kansas City School of Law (2004) [Online February 4, 2009] <http://www.law.umkc.edu>.

Loos, Anita. *Gentlemen Prefer Blondes -and- But Gentlemen Marry Brunettes: The Illuminating Diary of a Professional Lady*. New York: Penguin Classics, 1998.

Loos, Anita. *Kiss Hollywood Good-Bye*. New York: The Viking Press, 1974.

Marion, Frances. *Off with Their Heads: A Serio-Comic Tale of Hollywood*. New York: Macmillan, 1972.

Meade, Marion. *Bobbed Hair and Bathtub Gin: Writers Running Wild in the Twenties*. Philadelphia: Harvest Books, 2005.

Meade, Marion. *Dorothy Parker: What Fresh Hell Is This?* New York: Penguin Books, 2007.

Mencken, H. L. *A Mencken Chrestomathy: His Own Selection of His Choicest Writing*. New York: Vintage, 1982.

Menefee, David W. *The First Female Stars: Women of the Silent Era*. Westport, CT: Praeger, 2004.

Milford, Nancy. *Zelda: A Biography*. New York: Harper Perennial, 1983.

Miller, Nathan. *New World Coming: The 1920s and the Making of Modern America*. New York: Da Capo Press, 2004.

Moore, Colleen. *Silent Star Colleen Moore Talks about Her Hollywood*. New York: Doubleday, 1968.

Morella, Joe, and Edward Epstein. *The "It" Girl: The Incredible Story of Clara Bow*. New York: Delacorte Press, 1976.

Mowry, George, ed. *The Twenties: Fords, Flappers, and Fanatics*. Englewood Cliffs, NJ: Prentice-Hall, 1963.

Olive Thomas: Everybody's Sweetheart, 1894–1920 [Online June 6, 2009] <http://www.flapperjane.com>.

Paris, Barry. *Louise Brooks: A Biography*. Minneapolis: University of Minnesota Press, 2000.

Parker, Dorothy. *The Portable Dorothy Parker*. New York: Penguin Classics, 2006.

Pegram, Thomas R. *Battling Demon Rum: The Struggle for a Dry America, 1800–1933*. The American Ways Series. Chicago: Ivan R. Dee, Publisher, 1999.

Pollack, Howard. *George Gershwin: His Life and Work*. Berkeley: University of California Press, 2007.

Rodgers, Marion Elizabeth. *Mencken: The American Iconoclast*. New York: Oxford University Press, 2005.

Rose, Kenneth. *American Women and the Repeal of Prohibition*. The American Social Experience Series. New York: NYU Press, 1997.

Scopes, John Thomas. *Center of the Storm: Memoirs of John T. Scopes*. New York: Henry Holt, 1967.

Sinclair, Andrew. *Prohibition: The Era of Excess*. Boston: Little, Brown, 1962.

Slide, Anthony. *Early Women Directors*. South Brunswick, NJ: A. S. Barnes, 1977.

Snickle, Richard. *The Essential Chaplin: Perspectives on the Life and Art of the Great Comedian*. Chicago: Ivan R. Dee, Publisher, 2006.

Stenn, David. *Clara Bow: Runnin' Wild*. Lanham, MD: Cooper Square Press, 2000.

Vogel, Michelle. *Olive Thomas: The Life and Death of a Silent Film Beauty*. Jefferson, NC: McFarland, 2007.

Watson, Steven. *The Harlem Renaissance: Hub of African-American Culture, 1920–1930*. Circles of the Twentieth Century Series 1. New York: Pantheon, 1996.

Weissman, Dick. *Blues: The Basics*. New York: Routledge, 2004.

Weissman, Stephen. *Chaplin: A Life in Film*. New York: Arcade Publishing, 2008.

Whitman, Alden. "Chaplin's Little Tramp, an Everyman Trying to Gild Cage of Life, Enthralled World." *New York Times* (December 27, 1977) [Online February 8, 2009] <http://www.nytimes.com>.

Wollstein, Hans J. *Vixens, Floozies, and Molls: 28 Actresses of Late 1920s and 1930s Hollywood*. Jefferson, NC: McFarland, 2005.

Zeitz, Joshua. Flapper: *A Mapcap Story of Sex, Style, Celebrity, and the Women Who Made America Modern*. New York: Three Rivers Press, 2006.

Films

Gentlemen Prefer Blondes. Howard Hawks, director. 20th Century Fox, 1953. DVD, 2001.

Inherit the Wind. Stanley Kramer, director. United Artists, 1960. DVD, 2001.

"It" Plus Clara Bow: Discovering the "It" Girl. Clarence G. Badger, Hugh Munro Neely, and Josef von Sternberg, directors. Kino Video DVD, 2002.

The Jazz Singer (Three-Disc Deluxe Edition). Alan Crosland, Bobby Connolly, Bryan Foy, Buster Keaton, and F. Lyle Goldman, directors. Warner Home Video DVD, 2007.

The Joan Crawford Collection: Humoresque / Possessed *(1947)* / The Damned Don't Cry / The Women / Mildred Pierce *(1947)*. Curtis Bernhardt, George Cukor, Jean Negulesco, Michael Curtiz, and Vincent Sherman, directors. Warner Home Video DVD, 2005.

Mrs. Parker and the Vicious Circle. Alan Randolph, director. Fine Line Features, 1994. DVD, 2006.

The Olive Thomas Collection: The Flapper/Olive Thomas—Everybody's Sweetheart. Alan Crosland, Andie Hicks, directors. Image Entertainment DVD, 2005.

Pandora's Box—Criterion Collection (1929). Georg Wilhelm Pabst, director. Criterion DVD, 2006.

Index

About the Author

KELLY BOYER SAGERT is a freelance writer who has published biographical material with Gale, Scribner, Oxford, and Harvard University, focusing on athletes and historical figures. *Flappers* is the fourth book that Kelly Boyer Sagert has written for Greenwood Press. Previous books include *Joe Jackson: A Biography, American Popular Culture Through History: The 1970s*, and *Encyclopedia of Extreme Sports*. Sagert is a member of the American Society of Journalists and Authors, The Author's Guild, and the Society of Professional Journalists.